I CAN
HEAR
THE
CUCKOO

I CAN
HEAR
THE
CUCKOO

Life in the wilds of Wales

KIRAN SIDHU

First published in Great Britain in 2023 by Gaia, an imprint of
Octopus Publishing Group Ltd
Carmelite House
50 Victoria Embankment
London EC4Y 0DZ
www.octopusbooks.co.uk

An Hachette UK Company
www.hachette.co.uk

Distributed in the US by Hachette Book Group
1290 Avenue of the Americas
4th and 5th Floors
New York, NY 10104

Distributed in Canada by Canadian Manda Group
664 Annette Street, Toronto, Ontario, Canada M6S 2C8

ISBN 978-1-85675-500-9

A CIP catalogue record for this book is available from the British Library.

Printed and bound in Great Britain

10 9 8 7 6 5 4 3 2 1

Commissioning Editor: Nicola Crane
Senior Editor: Pauline Bache
Copy Editor: Jo Richardson
Design Director: Mel Four
Map illustrator: Jill Tytherleigh
Typesetter: Jouve (UK), Milton Keynes
Production Manager: Caroline Alberti

This FSC® label means that materials used
for the product have been responsibly sourced

To my mum and dad, Piari and Jalal Sidhu.

I miss you.

'In solitude everyone has to face himself'

Arthur Schopenhauer

CONTENTS

CONTENTS

Summer

Autumn

Winter

To the Sea

My Walk

Dai's Farm

Sarah - The
Farmhouse

Rod and G
(the barr

kittens
found here!

Little
Bridge

The Long Ba

THE VALLEY

Donna and Andy's Farm
& Caer Cadwgan B&B

Tess and Andrew's
Farmhouse

Jane's Farm

WELCOME

The Cambrian Mountains
(Mynyddoedd Cambria)

Sarn Helen Roman Road

Goblin Stone

Wilf's Barn

Derelict house

...ra and Si's
...armhouse

Cattle Grid

...oman
...l Forte

PROLOGUE

I had never been a walker and yet I had an inexplicable desire to put one foot in front of the other. The most important walks in life must be done alone, as solitary as a ghost.

I felt like skipping and hopping down to see Wilf to tell him the news that the cuckoo had arrived back in the valley, and it was me who had heard it. I was walking back from the walk Wilf did every night and I tripped as I rushed back to see him. I had taken a tumble and ripped my jeans. I brushed myself off and continued to walk and run.

It had almost been a year to the day that Wilf had first introduced me to the cuckoo, a bird that laid its eggs in another bird's nest; how curious. In those early days, I would never have recognised its call; a bird amongst birds.

But what was even more curious was that a Welsh farmer in his seventies, who had never left the small circumference of his existence, would be able to teach me so much about my own. A man in blue overalls, with a clothes peg instead of a top button, had gently, and unwittingly, ushered me into a spiral of thoughts. Our conversations, short. Our friendship, non-committal. I only saw him if I took my walk, but the conversations, even in their brevity, had made all the difference. I wondered what I had missed in life by thinking that the wisdom of others whose lives were different to mine could not have any bearing on my own life. How wrong I had been.

I

THE DAY EVERYTHING CHANGED

I know exactly when my mother died. It was 1am on Christmas Eve. I was at home having spent the evening at the hospital. I lay in bed in excruciating, unfathomable pain that made me howl like an animal, the pain so intense I felt like running into the road and getting hit by a car to release me from it; anything but this. My arms stretched out in front me, trying to hold onto my mother, life, God.

Then the phone rang and a scream, foreign to me, made its way out of my body. My husband, Simon, answered. And then gently put the receiver down. 'I told you she died!' I cried.

Like the pain she felt with me entering the world, I felt the pain of her leaving it.

The rest of Christmas Eve was spent trying to sort out all sorts of formalities that must be dealt with when a person dies: collecting paperwork from the hospital, the death certificate from the town hall and contacting funeral directors. All these tasks one must do seem cruel and inappropriate when you have been brought to your knees. Death is a formality with rules to adhere to.

Christmas Eve, my favourite day of the year, was spent collecting bits of paper confirming that my mother had really died. My life had gone into slow motion, and the rest of the world, which was frantically Christmas shopping, was running out of sync with my mine. I didn't understand how the town hall clock could strike midday, how people could still wish each other a 'Merry Christmas' and how the traffic lights could carry on changing. My mother had just left this world.

I cried unashamedly as I sat in a cafe drinking coffee while waiting for the town hall to open. I told the waiter that my mother had just died. He said the world was a dark place, and that my mother was now safe in the arms of the gods. I told the priest, who sat with three other priests for morning coffee, that my mother had died. He placed his hands on my head and gave me a blessing for strength, love and fortitude. It was Christmas Eve, a holy day, and nothing I had ever felt before had felt more of a spiritual experience than losing my mother. A lady in her late fifties, sitting on the opposite table with another lady having breakfast stared at me wistfully. I went up to her and told her that my mother had died in the early hours. Without looking at me, she said her daughter had died from cancer two months ago. Years later, I understood why the lady had purposefully looked away from me when I stood beside her. In me, she had recognised her own pain. I didn't care who I stopped and broke my news to. I was a drunk person that day in the cafe, stumbling around carrying my grief. I didn't care that it was Christmas Eve; death didn't care what day it was when it took my mother. I wanted to tell the world I was in pain and that I had just discovered a secret: the death of a loved one can trigger your own death.

I was certain that my mother had set up the people I had met in the cafe. She would have wanted the priest to lay his hands on me and to bless the solitary long walk that lay ahead: 'God, please bless my child.' She would have wanted me to seek some solace from the lady who lost her daughter to cancer: 'Kiran, you're not alone; this woman has also lost someone she can't live without. In the end, we all lose to death.' I believe my mother's spirit hung around in the cafe that day. She was there, and I felt her.

In the weeks that followed the death of my mother, I noticed 'mum' had turned to 'mother'. Gone was the colloquial 'mum'. She had become iconic and mythical; no longer tangible but an object of deep and painful longing. In death people become immortalised. Death elevates the deceased to foreign heights. The age-old mechanics of night morphing into day is a great divider of what you've had . . . and what you've lost.

My mind raced like an old home movie with years of film crackling away, frayed at the edges by time. I saw images of my mother collecting me from school, stirring pots in the kitchen, her warm smile when I visited, the way she looked in the mirror when doing her hair and her infectious laugh. These unremarkable, innocuous images had become inflictors of the greatest pain I had ever felt. A pain that silenced any other pain. These were the first tears my mother would not be able to wipe away. It was a great irony that the death of my mother was the most grown-up experience I'd ever had and there had been no other experience that had made me feel more like a child. I felt the End of all Ends. All the books from my childhood flew open to the last page: The End. The letters E, N and D made a beeline for me. My mother's life had Ended. It's strange how things make themselves known.

As still pictures of my mother swiftly flowed through my mind, I had become conscious and obsessive about the accuracy of my memory. I was aware that this state of all-consuming grief could create memories that I wish I had had, as well as the ones that I did have. And there was a fear, as time went on, that the shards of memories would become dormant and then inevitably fictionalised. It was important to me that I remembered my mother correctly and mourned what she was. I lived in the world of grief for years; a lonely world where grief became my friend, its existence the only other existence I was aware of. Grief had me in a headlock.

My mother's death made me acutely aware of the world turning on its axis. As the winter when she died passed, for the first time I really noticed the heads of daffodils and crocuses popping up. It seemed a cruel reality that life carried on, edging away from the day my mother died, slipping into a new season. It would always be winter for me. There would be no more creating new memories, the mother–daughter relationship I had now belonged in the deeps vaults of history. All that she owned were now artefacts. She was a part of history as much as

Anne Boleyn and the death of Socrates. My life divided into two parts: When Mum Was Alive (WMWA) and After Mum (AM). In the early days of losing her, friends and family said that I shouldn't allow the experience to define me. But some experiences do define us and we are changed from who we once were. I'm not sure why we are so committed to not changing, not evolving and remaining untouched by some of our greatest experiences. Some experiences do define us. And we do change.

I became obsessive about my mother's age at death: 62. I saw it everywhere – on front doors and on pages of books. The 3rd of March is the 62nd day of the year, Marilyn Monroe died in 1962, if you subtract 38 from 100 you get 62, 31 plus 31 gives you 62, Lottery numbers don't allow you to pick 62. I loathe 62.

In the early hours of Christmas Eve, my brother was nowhere to be seen, but my father, sister and my mum's siblings surrounded my mother's deathbed. I knew when my father said he would look after me and give me the love that my mother did, he wouldn't: he was incapable.

2

THE BIG DECISION

I never thought I could ever leave London. I love being swallowed by the city. I never imagined that one day it would spit me out. But as much as one imagines the future goings-on in one's life, one never imagines what actually happens.

I didn't put up a fight when I left. Years ago, I would have kicked and screamed. But years ago, my life had been intact. And it's a sign of maturity to see things as they are, and not how you wish them to be. London had become a Petri dish that cultivated pain. Before my big move, I ran away for a month to the bright lights of New York City to spend time on my own. I spent the days writing and watching a blur of people rotate in the world as I tried to find my place in it. I had become deeply sad.

It was not a desirable move but a necessary one. Desire had very little to do with it. In those years, in between the death of my mother and leaving London, the idea that I was in a position to desire anything felt unbelievably luxurious. There had been only one wish: to feel nothing and do nothing. And I wished it completely.

It was necessary to leave the toxicity of the city; my lungs had become clogged and acrid smoke restricted my breathing. My head was filled with angry words that flapped around in my head like a contaminated pigeon, and in the open cage of my mind it nested. Perhaps the strangest thing of all is that the toxicity and the pollution didn't come from the city but from my family.

There is a myth attached to family homes that they, like chocolate boxes, are filled with sweetness and all our hearts' desires. Family homes are fattened with love, filled with harmonious voices of those we share our blood with, forever connected by our lineage. But this isn't true of my own family.

It was when my mother died that my life reached a new epoch. Where there was once life and love, now existed a darkness in the people she left behind. A harsh bright light shone on all our broken parts. Links were severed, ties forever lost and all that blood that flowed between us flowed not because we were related but because we damaged each other so much. I was no longer able to fix myself and others and place us in a picture where we no longer belonged. The threads of the soft furnishings of our family home became unpicked and undone. It takes great strength to admit defeat and walk away. There is a story about families that people like to tell: you can't walk away from them. But you can. And I did. I had a visceral feeling that told me that I must pack myself up after what had been the great unpacking of me. Parts of me lay scattered. It was time to collect my belongings.

Something not only died inside me but had drastically left me: a sense of order and regularity. So in the end it was almost easy to leave London – it was the obvious thing to do. Never before had I felt my singularity in the world as I did in those days that followed the death of my mother. I was a red helium balloon released into the atmosphere, bumping into space debris, with nowhere to go. I was getting a bird's eye view of my life. Family who I thought would put their arms around me did the opposite, and I felt their treatment of me was atrocious, with snide comments down to outright judgements.

In the wake of my mother's death, I learnt to say 'no' to things that no longer served me well and to those who, no matter what, would always misunderstand me. I had always made excuses for the behaviour of some of my family members. Perhaps because, deep down, I had wanted to believe the toxic mantra: blood is thicker than water. I felt it was all I had left of my mother. In the end, all it does is keep you in abusive relationships, using blood lineage as an excuse. If you belong in an abusive marital relationship, most people encourage you to leave. So what is it about blood relationships that stop us from leaving? A toxic relationship is toxic whether that person is related to you or not. Why can't we tell the truth about our blood relationships? As soon as you cut off the toxic root of a blood relationship, the general sentiment is: 'You can't do that, s/he is your brother/ sister/aunt!' I began to understand that no matter how well tied we are to others, ultimately we're on our own. The two greatest events of our lives are experienced by ourselves: our birth and our death. We enter the world and leave the world alone. When you realise you are alone in the world, you do what is necessary to survive.

My surroundings no longer housed me sufficiently. I had learnt and seen too much to live contentedly. To stay put would mean to suffocate in all my yesterdays – like someone who had to be tube-fed after becoming paralysed; a slow drip-drip of life.

I ran to the hills. I slipped into the auditorium of silence. I chose fresh air to help me breathe. I chose the purity of farm animals over the people that hurt me. I chose to be in the proximity of strangers rather than the toxicity of my family. I decided to walk out of my old life, not to pick up the pieces and not to reassemble. I chose to listen to my heart over the cacophony that crashed in my brain like a jackpot of loose change. I chose things that I thought I would never choose, and strangely, they chose me.

There is a certain freedom when the tectonic plates of one's life shift. After the fall, the rabbit hole and the inevitable abyss, you walk alone. Free.

SPRING

3

ARRIVING AT CAER CADWGAN

Caer Cadwgan: a B&B that sits on a hilltop in Wales. Look through any window and you can see the countryside sprawling out like a mercurial green carpet between the grooves of the deep valleys.

It is here, soon after my mother died, that I spent Easter weekend. The night my husband, Simon, and I arrived was such a stormy godless night, even the windscreen wipers felt like giving up. Driving up the long winding road and into the hills, we must have gone past the same odd houses a dozen times and still couldn't find it. And of course, the mobile phone reception was non-existent; no phone call to ask for directions and no GPS. How can anyone live in such a godforsaken place? But I had wanted a break at a farm, and this smallholding was the closest thing we could find. I love animals: they exude purity and simplicity. Humans are complicated and gnarly. For me to stay grouped with humans now, after I had suffered so much pain at their hands, would be nothing but an act of violence. So I literally ran to the hills to all that was pure and uncomplicated.

If I was superstitious, I would have turned back. We weren't meant to find this B&B; the elements were against us. It seemed careless and stupid to carry on trying to find what didn't want to be found.

It took us more than an hour to find it, up a small nondescript dirt path. Later on, we would find out that we had passed the B&B many times in a perpetual loop. Under the cloak of darkness, the countryside was featureless; no obvious turning points, just tiny, winding roads that made me breathe in just passing through them. And then, out of nowhere, out of the blackness, a cow appeared in front of the car, its giant head right in front of our windscreen. I screamed. The cow had obviously escaped from a field. We stopped the car, as there was no way we could drive past it – the road was barely the width of our car. And the cow wouldn't budge. After about ten minutes, the cow jumped over the hedge and we were free to get lost again.

The B&B consisted of two outbuildings attached to the main house; a medium-sized country dwelling. The lights were switched off in the farmhouse, as it was after midnight. An outside sensor light illuminated the door of our B&B revealing the name of the room, Willow. We parked our car in front of an old tractor that sat in an open shed. Standing outside the car, I tried to look beyond the shed. But there was very little I could see; I was looking out into an infinite black hole. In the city, the night sky is an inky blue, but here, the sky was as dark as a bad man's soul.

The light of day showed me what had been hidden by the covert night. So much green, so many shades; tree-lined hills; a dog barked in the distance; someone was using a chainsaw somewhere; farms that looked like Lego were dotted around and there were forests full of secrets. Somewhere in my childhood I had once created this very picture; a collage using an assortment of pasta depicting a country scene. How funny that it should present itself to me now.

Easter morning, still in my pyjamas, Simon and I walked to the breakfast room, full of pictures of sheepdogs and farm animals alongside photos of children. A couple of the kids who featured in the photos popped their heads in to say hello.

Donna, a jolly woman with a broad smile, came in with a full Welsh breakfast: 'Did you sleep well?' she said in a thick Somerset accent. 'What a night it was last night! Sorry about the children. They know they're not allowed in the breakfast room when we have guests.'

I enjoyed watching her; the way she made herself present, moving things around the table, squirrel-like, making sure everything was just so.

Since that dreaded day that changed everything, I inhabited a world of silence. Silence was a womb that I existed in; cushioned by amniotic fluid, no words could hurt me here. Words like 'cancer,' 'metastatic', 'there's nothing we can do', 'terminal' and then 'I'm so sorry.' I only used enough words necessary to move the day along. Grief had silenced me. So I cannot say what made me spill out the contents of my heart to a complete stranger again as I had on Christmas Eve in the cafe. Perhaps it was the stars; the storm; Easter? My heart lay on the breakfast table like a Rubik's cube begging to be solved. But no one wants to eat heart for breakfast. 'My mother, she died, not so long ago. I feel rather lost.' Simon stretched out his hand to grab mine, which sat languid on the table. My darkness never perturbed Donna; in a fair exchange, she showed me hers. Holding onto a tea towel, she looked maternal and perfectly suited to this room that exuded warm domesticity. 'These children are my grandchildren. My daughter cannot look after them, so they live here with me.' She half-smiled; a knowing smile. She carried on with her story . . . two years ago she left Bath to offer the children a new life in the arms of the Welsh countryside. 'Family hurt us sometimes, don't they?' It was as though she could read my mind. My eyes welled up. Donna suddenly became jolly again. 'There are some things in life that can break us, and that's the truth. The only thing we can do is carry on, even when we feel as if we can't. What you have to remember is that we make our own family in life. People say life is what you make it. And that goes for family too.'

Simon got up, stood behind my chair and put his arms around me. 'She's had the most horrendous time,' he said.

Donna smiled at Simon: 'She'll get through it, we always do. And she has you. Let me know if you need anything else. And come and see the animals after you've eaten.'

We all politely smiled at each other and then Donna disappeared into the kitchen again. And in those simple exchanges, a connection was made. Maybe people find each other in the midst of their sadness, like fog lights on a stormy night.

After breakfast, still in pyjamas and wellies, I stood out in the spotlight of a sunny day. Donna's three grandchildren jumped on bicycles and an eight-year-old girl showed me around the mini farm: Rosie (horse); Penelope and Babe (pigs); Mavis, Myrtle and Vince (goats); sheep and chickens. And then there was Larry, a week-old orphaned lamb that needed bottle-feeding.

On that Easter morning, I sat on a garden bench looking out onto the wild countryside, bottle-feeding a little lamb that Donna had placed in arms which had closed since my mother died. I was missing a layer of skin – I could feel everything. The sun burned a little too brightly and the heartbeat of the lamb raced with mine. I felt a strange affinity with the lamb; motherless; in need of nurturing and vulnerable. I was drawn to all things broken.

'Would you like some biscuits?' asked Donna's granddaughter, standing right next to me. I didn't want to let go of Larry, so I declined the kind offer of a chocolate digestive. The girl sat bedside me on the bench: 'Do you like our farm?'

I waited a few moments before I answered; her simple question made me think.

'Yes. Yes, I love it,' I finally said. And I did.

'Are you going tomorrow?'

'No, I'm here for another two nights.'

'Will you come back?'

Donna arrived from inside the house. 'Leave our guest alone. She's on holiday and she doesn't want you bothering her.' The girl got up to leave.

'Oh, please stay.' I was enjoying the girl's company.

'Well, if you want her to go, just say. This one can talk forever,' Donna smiled and winked at me.

'Would you want to live here?' the girl asked.

Without even thinking, I said: 'Yes, I could live here. Will you look after me, show me how to live in the countryside and teach me about all the animals?'

'I will! Nan says I'm good at feeding the pigs and Rosie.'

'I can see you are! You're brilliant!'

'I think you're lovely. I want you to stay! Please stay!'

'I'd love to stay. Thank you.'

It was as simple as that. We would move to Wales. Within six months we found an old renovated barn. We made further renovations while we lived in London, which took us a year to do. And then we moved in.

4

A TIME FOR EXPLORATION

The spring we moved to Wales was a season of exploring. It's a very human instinct to want to explore; it's why we have populated the Earth so successfully. Curiosity took us to the moon.

The Llanddewi Brefi Road is mountainous with a 20 per cent gradient that takes you over the mountains and into the next valley, the Afon Twrch river valley, then straight down to Ffarmers village. It is this road, one fine spring day, that we travelled along. We snaked ourselves through the mountain range: our road less travelled.

I had never seen such barrenness. I don't think I had ever really *felt* a place so much – in joy or in happiness. I'd never been to a place that evoked so much solitariness in me or demanded so much of me. It's possible that some places hold you to ransom until they have taught you all you need to know. Wild and remote, it was strange that my new home was only down the road from this world that seemed so closed.

Driving up the tight and dusty single-track road, an array of different grasses hugged onto the sides, as if they were a welcoming fanfare. Words by John Greenleaf Whittier fluttered into my head like a butterfly:

> Flowers spring to blossom where she walks
> The careful ways of duty;
> Our hard, stiff lines of life with her
> Are flowing curves of beauty.

Heather, ferns, daffodils and bright yellow gorse. I realised how little knowledge I had of the various different bushes, rushes and grasses. I was unable to name most of them. It made me feel so 'city'. But sometimes, when you come from a different place and you feel contrast so acutely, you have your optimum chance of learning. My father once said to me, to learn anything, you must humble yourself first and admit you don't know something.

For all its remoteness, occasionally we would come across a few odd houses scattered around, some old working farms in the distance with outbuildings that looked like they belonged in the picture books of my childhood. When I was a child, we had a school visit to a farm. I remember seeing pigs and sheep and being thrilled. And I walked through an apple orchard and magic placed its hands on me. At the end of the day, we were asked what our favourite farm animal was, and we were then given a postcard of that animal. My postcard had a picture of pigs.

Driving up the mountain range, we spotted an old stone church with 1838 carved above the door. We passed a beautifully decorated house with old stone walls with protruding daffodils. A large brown alpaca stood proud on top of the daffodil wall. Further on, a makeshift sign said: 'Peacocks crossing – drive slowly'. We didn't see the peacocks, but we heard them. The peacock is the national bird of India, where my heritage is, and on holidays there I had heard their calls. How funny to hear this strange and exotic sound in what seemed like the deepest part of Wales; a mishmash of the foreign and familiar.

Horses ran alongside their new foals in dusty pens that belonged to a nearby riding school. Jersey cows walked alongside their calves and, of course, there were lambs – and they were jumping for joy. Spring had never felt so pure. The countryside is not quiet, not for those who really listen. There is an abundance of noise: horses, cows, bees, lambs and birdsong. It was the sound of life and the sound of being alive; just like the sound of a human baby being born, screaming itself into existence. Nature is the human whisperer.

What I really noticed in the spring was how much the very young lambs were like the young of humans. Driving through the valley you would always see little gangs of the youth of sheep getting into mischief. They would be racing with each other up the hills and then tumble around almost embracing each other. They would dance around rocks and then stand on boulders, as if they were kings of the Earth. And then you would see them annoy their mothers by greedily suckling on them. Occasionally, the mothers would try and kick them off. They would leap and hop, and looking at them you would think no animal could be happier than a lamb in spring.

On some parts of the drive, on the left and the right, stood a forest of huge pine trees that held the sky up, like pillars of a cathedral. It's this cathedral that I would gladly bow down at; one couldn't help but feel a prayer here. A few stumps made me think that perhaps the locals came here to pinch the trees for Christmas.

From a distance, it's clear to see the difference in landscapes between cultivated land and barren land. It's as apparent as seeing two oceans that meet but do not mix. The cultivated land has a rich greenness, and looks pristine and manicured. Beside it, the uncultivated land looks barren and brown. It's an explicit picture of how things can flourish if we give them our attention.

All this exists less than eight miles from my new home, The Long Barn. When I'm doing something as everyday as watching TV, I will suddenly, for no reason, be jolted by remembering that all this lives and breathes a stone's throw from my house; this wild and barren otherness, a giant in moss green. Any reservations that I might have had about being a non-white person in a white environment instantly feels insignificant. Because being surrounded by timeless things like nature and Roman roads really does make one feel insignificant. We recognise our finitude when we are standing next to a mountain or the sea. There is a certain humility that fills us when we stand in ancient woodlands.

Here, in the wild countryside, I am happy to feel my insignificance. I had felt the wrath of life for so long that I was glad to shift the focus of my pain to something clearly far greater than it.

5

MY NEW ENVIRONMENT

The Cambrian Mountains where I now live have Roman roads, a Roman fort signal station, Roman and Victorian gold mines, as well as Bronze Age and Iron Age settlements and extensive wildlife.

If you walk up my steep drive, turn right onto the single-track road and walk alongside the Cynon Valley, you will eventually reach a T-junction with a Roman road known as Sarn Helen. It's named after Saint Helen, thought to have been a daughter of the Romano-British ruler Octavius. Turn right and a steep walk takes you to the head of the valley, 400 metres above sea level. At the top, on the right-hand side, you will see Careg-y-Bwci ('Goblin's Stone'), thought to have originally been a Bronze Age circular burial mound with what appears to be standing stones. It's an important archeological site that has revealed Iron Age remains and clear evidence of it being a Roman signal station. It stands on a prominent point in the mountains with a wide panoramic view, with the Brecon Beacons plainly visible to the east. Looking west through the valleys, you can see coast belonging to Cardigan Bay.

The Cambrian Mountains are one of the more remote parts of the British Isles, described by writers in past centuries as 'the green desert of Wales'. They include the sources of the River Severn, the River Wye and the local river, the Tiefi. The land is primarily used for upland farming; mainly hill sheep farms and forestry, with many farmers specialising in rare breeds, such as alpacas and Mangalitsa pigs. There is small-scale silver, lead and gold mining from centuries gone by. The community is mostly of Welsh heritage and Welsh is the primary language.

This area is recognised as one of best dark sky sites in Europe. The Milky Way can be seen stretching across the sky from horizon to horizon from autumn onwards. In the midsummer night sky, you can see noctilucent clouds. If you know where to look, the Andromeda Galaxy and a number of the Messier objects can be seen with the naked eye. Some of the best sunsets in Britain can be experienced here.

Rare species of wildlife live in the Cambrian Mountains. The region is home to a total of 15 priority habitats, all of which are included in the UK biodiversity plan. It has six separate nature reserves. Red squirrels, cuckoos, adders, wild horses, ospreys, slow-worms, otters and black grouse are some of the wildlife that can be spotted here. The mountains saved the red kite; it was the bird's last refuge in the British Isles. Since the 1950s, a programme of breeding and protection has encouraged these birds and there are now over a thousand breeding pairs.

The area has many alternative and biodiverse farming methods, with farmers introducing the idea of 'rewilding' to their land.

On the western part of the mountain range is the Cors Caron National Nature Reserve, an area of wetland in the flood plains of the River Teifi. This area includes the most intact examples of raised peat bogs in Britain, up to 10 metres deep, which have built up over the last 12,000 years. It is home to countless species of butterflies and dragonflies. You can spot an adder, hen harrier or osprey here. Fifteen miles west, you will find yourself on the beautiful, unspoilt Cardigan Bay coastline. Many grey seal colonies and pods of bottlenose dolphins can be viewed from the Wales Coast Path.

The woodlands in this area are often referred to as 'upland oakwoods', or more generally as Celtic rainforest. Sadly, the native forest that previously dominated this landscape only survives in small fragments totalling around 2–3 per cent of the area. Nevertheless, those ancient woodland habitats that do exist contain rare tree, moss and lichen species.

Within this mountain range, it is man that is the rarer of the species.

6

THE SLAUGHTER OF PIGS

We had moved across the valley from Caer Cadwgan, the B&B that I had once been a guest of. From any window from the south side of my house, you can see Caer Cadwgan. Although somewhat camouflaged, if you know where to look you can see it quite clearly perched a short way below the hill. In the winter, when the trees have lost their leaves, it's plain to see. Especially if the fire's on and sinuous smoke snakes through the chimney.

In those early days, when I missed London, looking at Caer Cadwgan was a source of comfort. If the countryside felt a little too still or a little too quiet, I knew there was life in that house; people with tales to tell and lives that I knew. And people who knew me. I wasn't just a ghost leading an undocumented life in the wilderness. Donna would later joke that we should have a zip wire cutting across the valley connecting our homes.

One sunny Saturday morning I sat in Donna's kitchen. It's one of those lived-in country kitchens where all the lives of the residents are played out. Trays of eggs with bits of feathers laid by their own chickens sat on the sideboards and wellies were thrown by the front door. And there was always something delicious being cooked or baked.

'Kiran, you must be tired,' Donna said, handing me my second coffee. 'I got up to go to the loo in the middle of the night and saw your lights were still on. It's like the Blackpool lights looking at The Long Barn!' The truth was, Simon was away in London, and I felt scared of rattling around on my own in The Long Barn. I didn't mind being on my own in the city; I rather enjoyed it. But the countryside felt too silent for me. So I kept the lights on, too afraid to be left alone in the dark.

A man I had never seen before walked into the kitchen. He was wearing blue overalls. He said a gentle 'hello' by nodding his head and had a whisper of a smile.

'Fancy some toast, Ernie? Take a seat and I'll make you a coffee and a bit of breakfast.'

Donna was always feeding people. I think that's one of the nicest things about her. One of the sincerest things anyone can do for someone is feed them.

'Ernie's come to slaughter the pigs, Kiran,' she said nonchalantly.

At times I would get reminders that I was now living in the countryside and things were different, and this was one of those times. Ernie sat quietly eating his toast and drinking his coffee while staring out of the open kitchen door. There was a gentleness about him, an aura of contentment, a sort of serenity that one finds in old country folk.

The moment I found out the pigs were getting slaughtered, the morning felt different: epic and solemn.

'Ernie, could I please watch?'

I shocked myself; I would never normally ask such a thing.

Donna made a face, 'Do you really want to, Kiran? I wouldn't.'

Ernie nodded, 'Yes, if you like.'

He asked me if I had seen an animal get slaughtered before and looked concerned when I said I hadn't. He finished off his coffee and toast and went outside and put on a white plastic apron.

I can't tell you exactly what made a squeamish person like me want to witness a slaughter. Perhaps it was the simple fact that I didn't want a watered-down version of country living, for the city girl to have to be protected from the truth of the ugly parts of life. I didn't need protecting. I had already seen the brutal parts of life. I had witnessed the slow death of someone I loved and how, sometimes, we can wish for death; that death can become the pacifier and the saviour – the thing we will for the most. The last few years had opened me up to a different way of being and I was open to life in a whole new way. Being a meat-eater, I didn't think it was right that I should turn away from the realities of eating meat. I was an active participant in this chain of events – why should I have the luxury of turning away? City people are so detached from the whole process of where our meat and produce come from. I no longer wanted to think of meat coming from aisle No. 9 in

Sainsbury's. I felt morally obliged to watch something that I played a part in.

Ernie talked me through the whole process as he put his plastic gloves and apron on. He would occasionally look up to see if I was OK and we would both give each other a reassuring smile, a sort of handshake between the city and the country dweller. This gentle, courteous, softly spoken man with kind eyes was about to kill two pigs; pigs that I had once helped keep alive by feeding them leftover rotten fruit and veg. Pigs, my favourite farm animals since I was a kid. I remembered that postcard I had of pigs from the school trip to the farm. It seemed somewhat incongruous: kindness and brutality; a wolf in sheep's clothing.

But why would I think Ernie was any more of an ogre than me just because he did the killing and I just did the eating? Why should he be labelled the murderous one? In the UK, we sell foie gras but don't make it because we think the act of force-feeding an animal to enlarge its liver is barbaric. And it is. But to sell it and then make a judgement on the nature of the product is a bit like knowingly purchasing stolen goods but refusing to do the dirty deed of stealing because you think stealing is bad. I was just as 'murderous' as Ernie. If I want to eat meat, I should face facts and watch the slaughter. I felt brave; I had always ripped off life's sticking plaster and stared at the wound. For better or for worse. If you don't look, reflect and learn from experience, it no longer becomes an 'experience' – it's just something that's happened to you.

Andy, Donna's husband and a trained butcher, was on site helping Ernie with anything he needed. We were prepped on what would be done. The pigs would take a bullet to their head inside the horse trailer, which was pulled up by the side of the house. A pig was escorted to the horse trailer where Andy had laid out a carpet of hay. Ernie went inside the trailer and the sound of trotters slipping around made a tremendous noise. For me, this was the most harrowing part; the sound of a struggle. And then the pig's throat was cut, and all the hay turned red; a release of life and the end of life. I had never thought of blood as being a symbol of both: life and death.

The pig was taken out of the trailer and then placed on a trestle table that Andy had set up. Boiling water from a stainless steel teapot was poured over the dead beast. Beside Ernie, there was a constant supply of boiling water from a dustbin-sized steel bin. The boiling water softened the pig's skin, allowing Ernie to scrape the pig's hair with a brush and a blade. I was amazed at how easily the hair could be removed; as easily as peeling a banana. With the pouring over of boiling water, the smell of boiling flesh filled my nostrils. Once the hair was removed, pinkish skin was revealed and the pig looked familiar in its nakedness. The animal's hairy head was still intact when it was strung up by its hindlegs. I expected this part to feel clumsy and brutal, but it wasn't. Ernie had so much skill and grace that I was amazed at how a killing could look so easy and inoffensive. And then Ernie slit the pig in the middle, from hindlegs to throat, in one easy incision. Next, the entrails were removed – kidneys, liver, heart and intestines – mostly in one piece. It was strange looking at this collection of parts, so familiar and yet so gory. Only 30 minutes ago these parts had all been working collectively, keeping the beast alive. I thought about the workings of my own body; one day, they too would stop working. The head was finally removed, and what was left was recognisable as something I had seen in butcher's shops in London.

It had all been so quick. From the pig wandering around in its pen to being killed and butchered. But that was life; fragile, brutal and flickering. In Ernie, I felt a sense of humility. When he took his gloves and apron off, it was as ceremonial as removing a cloak; no longer the Grim Reaper. The deed was done and a strange quietude filled the air, as if acknowledging the falling of a great beast. I walked away thinking about how much respect was present during the slaughtering; a respect for the animal, for food, for life. Strange thoughts to walk away with after seeing a living being killed. But that's what I thought and still think. There was no jeering, no attitude of 'I won the prize' that humans often have. There was no 'I am better than the beast' display. There was a matter-of-factness about the whole thing. It was this attitude that allowed me to watch something that had the potential to upset me.

I spoke to my London friends that day and told them what I had witnessed. 'How could you?!' Some friends wondered how I could ever eat bacon again, as if no meat-eating person is aware that something has to die before it reaches our plate. Later that year, I ate the pig that I had once fed and then watched being slaughtered. It was now a sweet and sour belly of pork. And I did a strange thing, some would say. I thanked the pig for helping me recognise the circle of life, sacrifice and how life is full of irony. I also helped Andy make sausages from the pigs. I'd be lying if I said I didn't feel some oddness with such a hands-on experience with an animal I had once known, but I knew where my dinner had come from – and it wasn't aisle No. 9 in Sainsbury's.

Indian women, my mother's generation especially, sacrifice so much of their own happiness for the family. It's as though their happiness doesn't matter; their happiness can only exist vicariously, through husbands and children. I no longer craved just the extraordinary – I craved everything, in all its beautiful and ugly glory. I wanted to see the beginnings, the ends and all the middle bits of life. I didn't want to miss a thing.

7

THE LONG BARN

The Long Barn started life two hundred years ago as a milking parlour for cows in the Cambrian Mountains, Mid Wales. It sits at the bottom of a lush valley as if the very hills have regurgitated it.

As soon as we saw The Long Barn, we knew it was for us. It needed a lot of work, but I felt there was something quite magical about it. And it was close to Donna's house, which was important for me. We stayed in London while it was being renovated. When we bought it, we stripped it until it looked derelict and dangerous: hanging wire and loose tiles and floorboards. It felt especially abrasive because I longed for a cocoon to rest in; a container I could pour myself into. And all I could feel were sharp edges.

The renovation cost more than we had expected. We had moved from a small two-bed London flat to a five-bed house. We didn't have the money to furnish it, so we decided to look for old, cheap furniture on the local community Facebook page. We would have to upcycle – make good of what was available.

It was a rather fascinating insight looking at what people sell: wedding dresses; salt and pepper pots; lanterns; old car tyres; doors; candlesticks; curtains; sofas; wooden boxes; mugs; armchairs and wardrobes. Artefacts from people's lives surplus to requirement, no longer needed. And sometimes you find what you need. My knowledge of upcycling was at its most basic. I watched the odd TV show that made something from nothing, and that was it. But if we were to furnish the house, it was what we must do – tap into our creativity.

When we did find things we needed, trying to find the location of their whereabouts was a complete nightmare. In Wales, if you're off the main roads, so not on town roads, roads don't have names. Out in the sticks, it's the houses that have names. And these are Welsh names, a language with not many vowels – names that we now found we couldn't pronounce. A postcode can cover 2–3 square miles. We found that often a GPS would take us to the middle of nowhere in a place with no real landmarks. With the reception failing us most of the time, we were unable to call the person to ask for directions. We were sent to remote fields and up tiny, winding roads. We were collecting old bits of furniture from old farms and country houses where the landmarks were trees and hedges. When we did eventually find our destination, it was an education in Welsh hospitality. The Welsh are chatty and friendly people who have a lot of time for others. On one occasion, when we picked up a chest of drawers, we were given slices of lemon drizzle cake that had just come out of the oven.

One day, in daylight hours, we bought an old drinking cabinet from a ramshackle farm. Entering the property, we could see Pygmy goats wandering the land, a pond with 12 ducks, cats and sheepdogs. It was a whimsical and charming scene that made me think of the inventor's home in the film *Chitty Chitty Bang Bang*. We had just driven into a storybook. I loved the shabbiness of it all. An old farmer came out of the house to greet us along with his son and daughter, who were probably in their twenties. The daughter was cradling a tiny kitten. They took us to the shed where the old drinking cabinet that we came to see lived. The shed was full of stuff: tyres, furniture, lawn movers. And there it was, an ugly-looking bit of old furniture that should have been thrown away a few decades ago. I bought it.

Our best find was a baby grand piano for £100 bought from a young farming couple who were moving house. Simon is a musician, so it was both a beautiful and fitting purchase. The lady wasn't happy to sell it, but they simply didn't have the room in their new abode. One night, this beautiful, elegant piano had been dismantled and delivered to us in a tatty old sheep trailer by four burly farmers. The next day, Jimmy, a man in his seventies from the down the road and a keen musician, popped his head in: 'I saw you had a piano delivered!' he exclaimed. How Jimmy knew that a piano had been delivered under the cloak of darkness I don't know. But it was then that I realised how successfully news permeates across the valley. If you sit on the balcony of The Long Barn, you will be amazed at the sounds you are able to hear. I can hear Donna's sheepdog, Jake, barking, and across the valley someone is using a chainsaw. Hannah and George, who live a ten-minute walk away, are repairing their tin roof. I can hear that Hannah, who is on the roof, has dropped her hammer and is swearing profusely. We are all dotted around this valley, our lives facing each other. Noise travels differently in this natural amphitheatre; a concave steel drum, bouncing off the sounds of our lives. When people say that the countryside is quiet, all that means is that it's absent of city noise; the countryside has its own noise. And just as the sound of our lives echoes in the valley, I came to understand that this is also how news travels here.

I didn't know that upcycling old furniture could feel so much like therapy. But it all seems rather obvious now; restoring something tired and making it feel brand new. But not all discoveries are epic, and we don't always hunt them out like Scott and Antarctica. Some things come to us imperceptibly. I discovered that the feeling you get from the process of creating is almost the converse of the feeling of loss. Bringing something to life is the opposite of losing something, and I had the ability to bring something to life. In the last six years, so many things had happened to me that I had no control over. Someone I can't live without died. And people who I thought cared about me hurt me. I became acutely aware of how vulnerable I am to the existence of others. For years, I had been wandering in this dead-end powerless place like a ghost in a cul-de-sac.

But creating and shaping The Long Barn gave me freedom and control. I chose colour schemes and put together mood boards – a coming together and a gathering of things. There is power in dexterity; we are able to make whole new worlds that didn't exist before, a power usually attributed to deities. We are omnipotent creatures when we create. Suddenly, I could exist in a world of my creation; immerse myself in newly written song lyrics; breathe into the images of paintings that I chose to hang on my walls and bathe in rooms I could call my own.

The act of creating is an innate part of our humanity. Our innovation has given us the ability to inhabit the most challenging of environments. The Korowai tribe, from Indonesia's southeasternmost region of West Papua, live in treehouses, and then there are Inuits. It was of some comfort to me to think of all these faraway people, in faraway lands, making homes in the most unlikely of places. If someone could make a home from trees or ice, a city girl like me could make a home in the country. Perhaps my life wasn't meant to be lived in one place? I decided that, after years of being plagued by sadness, I must present myself to the world again; we cannot sit in the comfort of our living rooms all of our lives.

Even though innovation and creating are inherently human traits, we seem to harness our creative desires only once we get to the end of our schooling. We are told that no one makes money from art, so we leave the act of creating to those who are brave enough to dream. We carry on with our 'sensible' adult lives, neglecting our artistic selves, muzzling our need to put pen to paper, brush to canvas. And so we never really get to acknowledge the power of creation. We fear we cannot paint or write unless we're Monet or Stephen King. We leave creative pursuits to the music makers and those we consider eccentric. But we needn't be geniuses to create.

The old brown 1940s' drinking cabinet I bought from the ramshackle *Chitty Chitty Bang Bang* farm was my first project. In years gone by, I would have thrown it on top of a bonfire. But I stripped it, sanded it down and primed it. It is now a beautiful duck egg blue with gold features, and it looks like a Fabergé egg. An old chest of drawers that had seen better days is now sage green with handsome gold handles. Some pretty wallpaper from my London home lines its drawers; part of my old life is sitting in a drawer.

I didn't always have successful purchases. I saw an old dressing table being sold for the dirt-cheap price of £10. As always, it took us some time to actually find the place, and when I saw the dressing table, it was awful. It had obviously been repainted a dozen times, and not very well. It had fallen apart many times, it was clear to see, looking at the joins. The elderly lady who owned it told me the story of how the dressing table had once belonged to an old aunt who had led a wild and glamorous life in Paris. When she pulled at the drawer, the force of the pull made the back of the dressing table drop off. I didn't want it but I was far too polite to say so. So we took this awful bit of furniture home and before we even got home decided that we would put it on the bonfire that we were going to have the next day. I was glad to see that the handles were actually good, shiny and new. I removed them and screwed them into my last creation, the sage green chest of drawers. And then it did go on the bonfire.

The Long Barn became as important to me as a paintbrush is to an artist. It was the beginning of my propagation.

8

WILF THE FARMER

Much is said about walking the road less travelled. And there is joy in the unexpected and unravelling of, well, who knows what.

Walking as such, though, has never been my thing, but what's the point of being in the countryside if you're not going to go for a walk? So I bought a pair of expensive walking boots and made it my goal to put one foot in front of the other. Which is how I came across Wilf, a farmer in his seventies.

Most days when I would go out for a walk I would see him tending to his sheep. It was a wholesome sight, a shepherd with his flock. There was something eternal about it, a man toiling the earth, as if this one scope of vision held all of eternity. It made everything else look so starkly ephemeral.

The first time I stopped and spoke to Wilf, he asked me what route I was taking. He was at the side of the road fixing the gate of a sheep pen.

'Are you walking all the way around? It's a good walk, that is.'

Those were the first words Wilf said to me; an utterance of a question. I liked this doing away with formalities of introduction. I found this to be very Welsh. We shared a valley, so there was no need to be introduced; we already knew each other.

'I'm just walking up the road and then back down again,' I said.

I didn't know the walk he was talking about, although later on it would become my regular walk.

'If you go up the road and turn left, that's an old Roman road. Walk past the cattle grid and at the top you'll come to the Roman settlement.'

He carried on with his directions and bits of information that meant nothing to me; I didn't know where the cattle grid was and I didn't know the nameless roads. If I couldn't put it in a satnav, did it even exist? His knowledge of the valley astounded me and I was envious of how committed he was to this one piece of land, as if it was the beginning and the end of him. I wondered how it must feel to be him, so anchored in life, when I felt so rudderless. He told me that the valley was cut in the shape of his heart. His words stayed with me as I carried on my walk. I thought of the amorphous shape of my own heart and wondered what form it would need to take for it to stop hurting.

One fine spring day, Wilf told me that the cuckoo would be arriving from Africa in ten days. Sure enough, in ten days the cuckoo arrived. And around the valley there was a mild yet palpable excitement upon its arrival. I was sitting on my balcony at The Long Barn when I heard it; its sound reverberated across the valley. And it was the sound of clarity. I expected the wild to be just that, wild. But it is ordered and precise.

I passed Wilf on my walk the next day. He was outside his shed putting water in huge containers for the sheep. He stopped what he was doing to talk to me.

'Did you hear the cuckoo?' he exclaimed.

'Yes! We were sitting on the balcony and we heard it. How long will it stay?'

He ignored me and carried on talking.

'They come all the way from Africa, you know. All that way, think of that, all the way from Africa.' He appeared to be laughing. But he wasn't laughing. He was crying. I wasn't quite sure what to do and wondered whether he was in some kind of physical pain. These were big salt-of-the-earth tears. A heaving of chest and shoulders.

I stood still, facing him, and for a brief few seconds I thought of the moment I was placed in, like a flashback but not a flashback because it was in the present moment. It was an acknowledgement of place and time in real time; a profound coming into consciousness; my place in the world. Me in a Little Red Riding Hood raincoat, standing on a directionless land, in front of a bawling old farmer that I hardly knew. And in this acutely conscious state, I didn't see or feel anything either side of the very moment that I was in. It was a nano-snapshot of my life. And I felt it, deeply.

'Some of the cuckoos never make it here. They die en route. Did you know that? They never make it.' Although he was crying, I could hear, quite clearly, what he was saying. Which is strange because I would always struggle a little with his thick Welsh accent, but I could hear him loud and clear now, even though he was bawling. The usual cacophony in my head had been silenced in this single snapshot of life, the flapping of the pigeon that had nested in my mind stilled. I heard Wilf as clearly as I had heard the cuckoo. 'That is sad,' I said. And I did feel sad. And in this moment of stillness, there was an honest exchange between two odd people who didn't quite fit in the world, who expressed a sorrow for all things that had fallen: cuckoos that crossed oceans; orphaned lambs; the people we loved whose hands we stopped holding; words never spoken and days that slipped into nights, never to return.

He said he looked forward to hearing the cuckoo arriving in April.

'A lot of people . . . locals and birdwatchers . . . come wanting to hear the cuckoo. But they don't stop long enough!' He raised his voice; a plea for the world to stop and listen. 'Sometimes, they don't even leave their cars. This makes me so sad. It hurts me that others don't get to enjoy it like I do. They will never hear the cuckoo.'

Uttering these words made him cry even more. As if his words had been locked in a birdcage and it was a relief to release them into the Welsh country air. And in the air that was heavy with the season of spring, his words fluttered and danced in between us. I didn't have an urge to move forward and hug him or give him a touch of the hand. I stood firmly rooted in the small place in the world that I occupied. I wanted him to be free to lament and sing his own birdsong. Such enormity of feeling should never be crowded. The distance between myself and Wilf gave space for words of sorrow to fall in between us. The contents of our hearts overflowed, and like seeds, they planted themselves in the fertile land between us. And all our oddities and idiosyncrasies were allowed to exist and be free.

Hearing the cuckoo marked the first day I stopped listening to the podcasts that usually accompanied me when I was out walking. They started to feel intrusive; why would I listen to someone talking when I could be listening to the rustle of leaves? Or the birds? Or the beat of my own raging heart? I'd be no better than the people who tried to hear the cuckoo by staying in their cars. The podcasts became emblematic of a world that never shuts up yet has very little to say. I would see Wilf working on his own in silence, but I was beginning to realise that he didn't work in silence. He was just attuned to a different frequency. The quieter I became, the more I could hear Wilf's world: sheep, frogs, crickets, swooping bats. It made me tearful; in the last six years, all I had heard was dissonance. The cries from the newborn lambs on that spring-day walk echoed my own internal cry. It was like a reverse origami, where the Earth, in a tight-fisted ball, was folding out rather than in.

Wilf continued to talk through all his tears, unperturbed by the openness and vulnerability of being alive. He was unlike any other farmer I had met, usually full of bravado and enhanced masculinity.

'The cuckoo will go back to Africa in June. And it lays its eggs in the nests of other birds, much smaller birds like the reed warbler.' The nests of other birds? 'Then once hatched, the cuckoo chick will throw out the other chicks or eggs in the nest. And sometimes the cuckoo will throw out the eggs to make room for her own in the nest. And the bird whose nest it is will feed the cuckoo's chick. And soon the cuckoo's chick is much bigger than the adoptive mother.'

I imagined a small warbler feeding a cuckoo's chick; both comical and disturbing. And with what was a huge revelation for me, Wilf went back to his daily chore of providing water for his sheep. And I was left with the image of a very small bird feeding a very large chick that wasn't its own. I bid Wilf farewell and carried on my walk up the hill.

My idea of 'Home' had always been challenged. A combination of not fully fitting in with my Indian heritage and then not feeling completely at home with members of my family. Although my parents were liberal, I was housed in a culture that was oppressive. With the death of my mother and the break-up of the family that was left, and then moving out of London, I had never felt more displaced. My mind fluttered back to the cuckoo, a bird that makes a home for its young in the nests of other birds. And then I thought about Inuits and tribes that make their homes of ice and in trees. And then back to the cuckoo, who expects other birds to rear its young. There were so many other ways of being.

I walked up the daffodil-lined road and the daffodils smiled at me. And I smiled back. Today my walk would be up to the top, until I came to the T-junction that Wilf said was with an old Roman road. And then I will turn back and walk home. On either side of me I could see Wilf's sheep and lambs running around. Wilf was known to have the prettiest sheep in the valley: Plynlimon Speckled-face sheep. People would joke that perhaps Wilf blow-dried his sheep, so clean and bouffant were their coats. He cared for his sheep as if they were his family. I could see a dot of a lamb running alongside its mother. And then I saw gangs of lambs racing together, startled by life; happy and free. I was surrounded by pure unadulterated joy. And it tasted like nectar. I wondered what it must feel like to be so sure of where you belong, like the dot of a lamb that ran alongside its mother or the lambs that ran in their little gang. I thought of Dorothy: 'There's no place like home.'

I started to think that perhaps *The Wizard of Oz* is as much about being away as it is about being at Home; being rooted and rootless; housebound and homeless. As a child, Dorothy's tale appealed to my sense of adventure and running away from the stuffy conservativeness of my culture. I couldn't stay at Home, not when I could step out and present myself to the world. Nothing happened indoors. The adventure was outdoors. Being at Home meant fitting into a mould with the smooth curves of submissiveness, not the challenging sharp edges of curiosity. In my formative years, I was reading books like *The Sceptical Feminist* by Janet Radcliffe Richards. My world was expanding and being challenged, and I began to see the injustices in everything.

I understood very early in my life that my mental health doesn't do well with strict parameters of being; my curiosity needs to breathe freely.

I reached the top of the road, the T-junction part of the road. I looked both left and right. To the right, the road went up a slow-inclined hill, so it disappeared out of view at the top into hazy spring sunshine. To the left, the road carried on straight with huge boulders on either side of it, placed by a giant. I was glad that I didn't have to make the decision this way or that way. I wouldn't know; I was a directionless wanderer in a Little Red Riding Hood raincoat, trying to love my lostness.

I turned around and walked back in the same direction that I had come. I was surprised at how the same road looked so different simply by walking the other way. All around me I could see trees in blossom, the greenest of grass and wild flowers. Apart from Wilf, I hadn't seen any other person on my walk. But there were butterflies, daffodils, bluebells, snowdrops and dragonflies – all stretching out before me. All these things that lay at my feet had been immortalised by the great poets and the dreamers. I wasn't ready for the big awakening of life, the start of a beginning, not when I could still feel so many ends. But I was in the wilds of Wales – I had no right to command the world to stop turning. It seems such a city-dweller's existence to presume that the world evolves around us, that it's at our beck and call with everything so instant. Wilf would never think the world revolved around him – the world moved, and he simply moved with it. I walked on and stepped out of my own ignorance.

He respected the rhythm and the timing of the earth. He was a willing and happy slave to it, as farmers are. They know it's futile to argue with nature. All that Wilf was surrounded by, the mountains, sheep and nature, all communicated one thing: the world is not ours to own.

It was strange that I longed for Home so much when growing up it was often a place of hurt. Perhaps it's a basic human need to want to belong and therefore have a Home. We all want the adventure of going out and being free. But we then want to come back to a Home that anchors us. In these stories about wandering heroes, from Dorothy to *The Odyssey*, the hero changes, touched by adventure. The Home remains solid and stable; it is the adventurer who has changed. On my walk, I understood that my need to belong wasn't greater than my need to be free. I wasn't willing to give up so much of myself in order to fit in with culture and family. How much of ourselves can we give up before we stop being who we are?

When the cuckoo arrived, and I had learnt from Wilf about its strange behaviour, I was beginning to realise that the concept of Home is mercurial, and subject to change, like everything else in life. There is so much focus on the home. We have catalogues dedicated to it; they have their own fashion. In India, I visited a home that consisted of one room, where a family of five lived, ate and slept. The beds they slept on were simply put up against the wall during the day. The idea of home for this family was at its most basic: shelter.

There is a Welsh word, *hiraeth*. Roughly translated, it means homesickness for a home that you can't return to or that never was. This foreign word, with no direct English translation, was a whisper of a prayer in my ear. It swam around in my mouth and I allowed my tongue to feel each letter – *H..I..R..A..E..T..H* – until it made a Home in my mouth. In actual fact, I've had many homes and have lived many lives. A part of me had always known that Home was never a fixed postcode. And now this brown city girl was finding Home in the wilds of the foreign Welsh countryside. We must have the courage to walk away from things that no longer serve us; it's folly to hang onto something that once was but no longer is. It takes insight and, albeit painful, acknowledgement to know the difference. I found Home in all the books that spoke to me, the snippets of conversations that stayed with me and the people that understood me. I have many homes. And I have lived many lives. Family is not always just the one that raises you.

I reached The Long Barn and thought how my conversations with Wilf were always just snippets of conversation: small talk. But small talk can never be called small when it unearths so much.

9

THE GIFTS OF EACH NEW SEASON

In the countryside, whatever season it is, you are occupied by the seasons that will soon follow. But not in a way that you're not present in the current season; there is an anticipation and mindfulness of what's to come.

In spring, we prepared for the autumn and the winter months. This was mostly done with one big activity: chopping wood for the wood burner. Food, water and warmth are basic and obvious human needs. But in all their obviousness, you don't know how divorced you are from how you acquire the basics until you are forced to chop wood for your need of warmth. I've never really thought about warmth. I only thought of it when I felt the absence of it, and then I put the central heating on. Warmth literally came from the touch of a button. I had never actively been involved in keeping myself warm until I moved to Wales and chopped wood. We bought branches and trunks from the local farmer, and the wood was delivered to us in a trailer pulled along by a tractor. It would usually be ash, oak and beech. And then the process would begin. The first task was to chainsaw the lumber into manageable logs.

The chainsaw was a beast that we couldn't do without. I wondered how, in days gone by, people used an axe. We had one and I tried chopping wood with it, just so that I could feel what it would be like to be a person from a different time. Once I managed to get it into the log, I found it almost impossible to get the wretched thing out. Using an axe was unbelievably difficult.

Once we had chopped the wood into manageable logs, we then used a hydraulic log splitter, a horrendously noisy machine that exerted the pressure of 7 tonnes, cutting the logs into further small parts. Like the chainsaw, this device was impossible to live without and had the potential to chop me in half. After the process of chopping the wood twice, once with a chainsaw and then with the hydraulic wood splitter, we stacked the wood in the wood store for the wood to season. This was the last part of the preparation. I always thought lighting a fire and keeping it lit was just a matter of throwing any old wood on it, but that's not the case. Wood needs to be seasoned properly in order for it to be good fuel. This is the process of allowing the sap to dry out of the wood, which makes it lighter and easier to burn. Should you pick up a log of seasoned wood and a log of unseasoned wood, the difference is clear.

Contrary to my belief, fires are not easily started and it takes effort to keep a fire burning. When we talked to friends in the valley, the conversation would frequently be about how much wood we all had in our wood store. This was often a lengthy topic of conversation. Wood was currency and the equivalent of checking out someone's impressive car in the city. And sometimes, on a rare occasion when we were running out, especially in the winter months, I would envy the fullness of a neighbour's woodshed. Something I never thought possible.

The most common wood we would get, from a farmer called Rhidian who lived a ten-minute walk away from us and looked after sheep, was ash. This was because of the problem with ash dieback, a fungal disease that has affected all species of the tree in Wales. The fungus attaches itself to the leaves and spreads through the branches, causing the tree to die. Symptoms of the disease are usually apparent in the crown of the tree, with the leaves turning black and falling in late summer rather than autumn. So this is why ash was the tree that was cut down the most for firewood.

Farmers don't just chop trees, they also plant new ones. No one is more aware and more respectful of the circle of life than a farmer. What we take away we must also return to the earth. I remember there was a time when Wilf had to chop a huge horse chestnut tree down because its roots had grown under a derelict building that was to be renovated. For months Wilf deliberated about chopping the tree: 'If I could only just move it, and change its location,' he would say. And this conversation of how he didn't want to chop the tree became as circular as the seasons. 'You know, I don't want to chop that tree down. If only I can find another way around this problem . . .' And then one day the tree was chopped, and you'd think Wilf had chopped his own arm off. The residents of the valley noticed that the tree had been cut down as if it had been the only tree standing. Conversations about how beautiful the tree had been and guesses as to how old it was were had. It was a tree amongst other trees, but its demise had been noted and mourned as though a great deity had fallen. The beginnings and the ends of life are so deeply pronounced in the countryside.

Nature is not interfered with thoughtlessly. For example, hedgerows can only be cut in early spring, before the birds start nesting, and the people who live here are mindful and respectful of this. Andrew, who is married to Tess and lives in the white farmhouse across the valley, just below Caer Cadwgan, is a gardener. And when the council asked him to trim some hedgerows that had become a safety hazard, a nearby resident, a woman in her late sixties, approached him. 'The birds won't be happy,' she said. Andrew assured her that he was just trimming a little from the top and there would be the minimum of disturbance. After all, it was the council that had instructed him and there was the issue of public safety, as the hedge had grown wild. The woman walked away only to come back ten minutes later. She stood in front of Andrew and sobbed loudly. At first, Andrew ignored the woman, unsure of what to do or say. After a few minutes had passed, concerned, Andrew asked her if she was OK and if she was in any pain at all. The woman informed him that when she walked away, she had left him to communicate with the birds, and they had told her that they were deeply unhappy with the hedge being trimmed. This she said had made her desperately sad and angry. She then informed him that she was a witch and he was a bad man for upsetting the birds. And because of this she had just put a spell on him. And then walked off. Andrew carried on trimming the hedgerow, but for weeks he worried he would wake up with a pig's tail coming out of his backside.

Even though we had central heating and all the other mod cons that made living easy, chopping wood for heat tapped into a real primal feeling, where thinking about winter filled me with a sense of foreboding. But I was excited by this gentle reveal of what might come; a harsh winter upon us, a hunkering down. When I first moved to Wales, Jane, a 70-year-old woman who lived on her own on top of the hill, came knocking on my door. She came bearing gifts of woolly jumpers and a scarf she had knitted herself.

'These will keep you warm,' she said. 'The winter months here are harsh – they get inside your bones.'

When I was kid, one of my favourite books was *Joseph and the Amazing Technicolour Dreamcoat*. I asked my mother for a coat just like Joseph's. Instead, she knitted me a scarf that had more colours than I knew the names of. It was my rainbow scarf. Just like the scarf this stranger was giving to me now.

There is an old derelict house that I walk past when I go for my regular walk. It has no roof and the walls are made from old crumbling stone; the place is no more than a ruin. I've always imagined that it must have last been occupied a hundred years ago. When I walk past the house, I think of the people that must have lived there. I wonder how they survived the harsh winters and what animals they kept, if any. But I was told that the house was actually occupied as recently as the 1990s. In it lived an elderly bachelor, Gwylyn, and his elderly sister, Tegwyn, neither of whom married. Gwylyn and Tegwyn lived without any electricity. When the weather was bad, they would bring their sheep in and sleep amongst them to keep warm. They had no car and would walk four miles to go to the local shops. One day, Gwylyn was found dead indoors amongst his sheep; it was winter and he had slept beside them to keep warm. And his sister was put in a care home in town. This was in the 1990s – not a hundred years ago.

The preparation for each season gave them character and a mythical quality. Although we were in spring, we were preparing for a merciless giant named Winter that would turn our skies steel grey. I felt closer to animals; the squirrels that hibernate, and all the other animals that prepare themselves for what lies ahead. This innate need to prepare – basic and primal – made me think I was no longer just part of the rat race, as I had been in London, but part of the whole animal kingdom. I was stripped of any human hubris that I may have had. Living in the city had thrown me out of orbit; the city lights had dazzled too brightly. Here, I walked the land, greeting each new season, my ear closer to the earth.

10

JANE THE CONQUEROR

In London, people who are alike stick together. In the countryside, people are stuck together whether they're alike or not.

Jane from the top of the hill, just above Donna and Andy's smallholding, lived in a higgledy-piggledly house with a bit of land. She had four alpacas, ten geese and three dogs. There was a touch of whimsy about her.

I would often find Jane sitting at Donna and Andy's house in the kitchen with a cup of tea, and that's how I first met her. There was always something quite frantic about her; a busyness, a sense of urgency. Escaped wisps of hair just added to this 'time waits for no man' quality to her. She was spritely, chatty and a whizz at a game of chess. She was a member of the local chess club that met every Thursday in the local coffee shop.

She would often drop into The Long Barn unannounced, open the kitchen door and shout, 'Hello!' I liked that in the countryside people just popped in. There was no warning call or text message. In London, there was always a back and forth of texts trying to find a time when a friend could 'pop in', when in actuality there was no 'popping in', just regimented planning of what was to happen and when. People moved much more freely here. When she would arrive, she'd have a tinkle on the piano while telling me a story of what had happened to her during the course of the week.

There was one day when her West Highland White Terrier, Tipi, prone to teasing the geese, almost drowned. No matter how many times Jane would scold Tipi, she would get too close and yap at the geese. Then one of the geese grabbed Tipi by the scruff of the neck and dragged her to the pond where the goose tried to drown the dog. Hearing the commotion, Jane rushed to the noise and jumped around screaming, making the goose drop the sodden dog in the pond. I hadn't known much about geese before Jane told me that story. I certainly didn't know they were that aggressive. I learnt that a flock of geese, nicknamed the Scotch Watch, guarded the warehouses of whisky distiller Ballantine's at Dumbuck, Dunbartonshire, protecting the whisky from thieves, for more than 50 years. White geese are said to have raised the alarm when Rome was attacked by the Gauls, thus saving the city.

Jane's other stories ranged from fixing a leak in the kitchen, the new shrubs she had planted or the apple sauce she had made. Often she would come with a jar, or whatever else she had baked, cooked or pickled. And we would talk about everything: politics, books, art, planting, love, clothes, life. And the more we spoke, the more I realised how many lives she had lived. She knew something about everything. She was like the Russian matryoshka dolls: a life within a life, within a life. Jane and the Russian dolls told the same story: we may only have one life, but in the one life we can live a great many.

This lively 70-year-old woman became a great source of inspiration for me. When I told her I wanted to learn the piano, she dropped off a book that had taught her how to play. And this was her general attitude in life; if you don't know how to do something, just look it up and then do it. 'Everyone is so afraid of failing in life,' she would say. 'Failing is as much part of life as succeeding is. The only time we really fail is when we don't try.' Being around Jane made me realise how much of a procrastinator I was in my own life. This woman who only a few years ago recovered from mouth cancer was capable of so much.

Jane watched YouTube videos for everything, simply because she wanted to be everything and do everything. She paved her own garden with a brick mosaic design, did her own plumbing, fitted and laid down flooring in her kitchen and chopped all her wood. She crocheted, stitched and knitted. Her cooking ability could have easily made her head chef at any restaurant. She had a spinning wheel to make skeins of wool from her alpacas, which she would then make jumpers and scarves out of. She was so many things and more.

One day I opened up to her about my family. She said something quite unexpected. 'You know, I have never wanted to have anything to do with my mother. We must live our own lives, Kiran.'

I nodded. 'Yes, I know all this is true . . .'

And as my words drifted off, she said: 'It is not our job to take on other people's rubbish. If people want to be miserable, let them. But we must not lose our own sparkle trying to fit in where we don't.' She was calm and logical in her approach to life. She was articulate with a no-nonsense attitude. After knowing all these things about her, I understood her almost frantic nature and why wisps of hair would always escape from her. She was busy being and doing. She had worlds to conquer.

My mother would have loved Jane. She admired strong and independent women. It's something that we both had in common; we enjoyed stories of women who had made themselves known in the world. And whenever I met such a woman, I'd tell my mum. I imagined the conversation I would have with my mother about Jane. I'd tell her about all the things she creates, and my mother would say, 'What an incredible woman' and then, 'Isn't she brave'. And then my mother would ask me to invite her over so that she could cook for her. My mother, like Donna, enjoyed feeding people. This imagined conversation with my mother, about Jane, made me feel sad. So many lost conversations.

Looking at Jane and me, you would think that our friendship couldn't exist deeper than mere formality of greetings, the lack of commonality separating us. But knowing her made me think about how much we miss in life by sticking to the people who are like us. Perhaps years ago I would have thought the same, that we would tread little common ground and therefore we wouldn't have much to talk about. Perhaps, if we both lived in the city, where people are in abundance, we wouldn't have spent enough time together to know that we enjoy each other's company?

It's strange that people assume that because they are worlds apart and orbit different planets they cannot get on, or that there is nothing that can be learnt from each other. The greatest myth and mistake is to assume that because someone is vastly different from you, they can't teach you anything of interest. What my dual culture of British and Indian has taught me is that, just because something is different from you, it doesn't necessarily mean it will always be estranged from you. When you grow up in two cultures, you innately know that there are multiple ways of thinking and being. I have always been presented with two rather contrasting viewpoints. You don't have to just look inside the box: look underneath it and around it. This cultural quandary, which may be disconcerting to some, is a cultural wilderness that I am happy to roam; the path I tread in life has a far more interesting terrain. I prefer my road to have bends than to be straight and narrow. 'This way or that way?' is a far better question than the instruction of a one-way street.

Humans have gone to great lengths to try and find alien life. It's one of the greatest questions of all time: is there life outside our planet? We are fascinated by the alien; the different, the quirky; beings that are so different from us that they are light years away. We hunt them out. We've spent trillions leaving our planet and shooting off into space to find all that's alien. And yet difference and alien sit beside us every day, but we recoil because suddenly we're afraid of the alien.

Jane and I were opposites in so many ways, which meant I had everything to learn. And Wilf existed on a planet that was even further away from mine. And yet our planets found ways to gently orbit each other, waltzing in space and time. And all this shed some light on the confused idea of Home that had gnawed away at me since I was a little girl. Just because a place is familiar to you, it doesn't always mean it's the place where you belong.

Jane had been widowed once and divorced once. She had been on her own for 35 years, which was why she was so fiercely independent. I had secretly hoped that, by the method of osmosis, some of her attitude about life would rub off on me. Knowing her made me acknowledge that there isn't much that I actually know. And I couldn't welcome this feeling enough; the feeling of being a blank canvas, my minuteness in the world, a beguiling strangeness that thrilled me. The world was wild and unfamiliar. And I wanted to befriend it.

One day, Jane met someone, a man who was a whizz at chess. And when she visited me, she was a girl of 16, as we all are at the beginning of love. He had five alpacas to add to her four and two dogs to add to her three. After a short courtship, at the age of 71, they got married one wet and miserable February morning, but to her it was the sunniest of days. She told me their future plans of driving around in her camper van, which she had renovated, and travelling until their hearts were full. Her new motto:

adventure before dementia; their new life together, a symphony of roses. They spent their days playing chess, planting, tending to their polytunnel, painting and drawing and playing with train sets. She had entered a new metamorphosis.

Jane became an inspirational figure not just to me but also to my friends in London, whom she had never met. They were bowled over by her joie de vivre: hers was a story of hope, optimism and vigour. And whenever my friends or I feel a little timid in the face of life, we all say the same thing: 'Do a Jane!' Be bold and dare to be free.

II

SPRINGTIME IN THE GARDEN

Spring was a time for activity, not just for the surrounding wildlife but for us too. It was a time for planting.

In early spring, we put seeds in a seed tray in the kitchen by the window where it was light and warm. We had capsicum peppers, everyday and beef tomatoes, aubergines, courgettes and basil. In the garden, we built raised vegetable beds made from old attic floor joists from when we had gutted The Long Barn. Something old made into something new. In the raised beds, we planted both heritage and everyday carrots, red and white onions, beetroot, lettuce, pak choi and spring onions. And most days I would wake up and look out of the window that looked out onto the garden to see all that had flourished.

Once the tomatoes matured in growth – tall and flowering – they were transported to the greenhouse and planted into bigger pots using our own compost made from rotting vegetables. Tomato seeds are so small, they barely exist. If you put them in your hand and then sneeze, you will lose them forever. Yet these tiny seeds pushed their way through the soil, determined to feel warmth, and grew tall and strong. It's exciting to wake up and see them adorned with yellow flowers, soon to be tomatoes. To witness transformations like this takes time and patience. Sometimes change is small and so nuanced that others will barely notice. You will have revolutions so quiet, there will be no fanfare. Huge tectonic shifts will be felt, unnoticeable to others; they will be blind to the tsunami that took you away. But for you, you woke up and everything had changed. You felt the Earth move while everyone else drank tea and talked about the weather. And you will be offended by their civility in the face of something so great.

It's a wonder how, whatever you give your attention to, becomes a world of its own, from a blade of grass to a garden pond. And for a short time in spring, our front garden was the only world I existed in. When we bought the property, it was everything but a garden. It grew wild, a veritable jungle. It had boulders, brambles, dock leaves, stinging nettles and wild trees and bushes – all overgrown. When the Long Barn was a milking parlour, the front garden would have been the courtyard, and at some point the ground had been turned over. But once we started digging, we discovered 200–300-kilogram boulders. We had to enlist the help of our retired farmer friend, Geraint, with a tractor, to move the huge rocks. Geraint always arrived with his old sheepdog, Bob. Everyone knew and loved Bob; he was so friendly. Locals say that when God made the world, the rock he had left over he dropped into our village, Cellan; it's so rocky here. This project, of making the garden look like a garden, was one of the toughest jobs. The whole barn seemed wild, even though it had been inhabited when we bought it. We had six wasp nests in the loft that needed to be professionally removed, and the loft was crawling with mice.

In spring we had a visitor, a grey squirrel that managed to eat its way through a 240-volt cable and some heating pipes. The electrics went bang. Amazingly, the squirrel did not electrocute itself but carried on making a home in the void of the flat roof, the extension part of the house, above the guest room. It is the red squirrel that is native to Wales, and considered an endangered species because of its declining numbers. It is threatened by the larger and more aggressive grey squirrel, so a number of farmers and individuals are licensed to help keep the population of grey squirrels down by shooting them.

Outside, we blocked off all the holes that we noticed in the soffits and replaced the old fascia boards to prevent the squirrel from coming and going. In the newly plastered ceiling, we had to cut holes so that we could get access to the chewed heating pipes. And in cutting a hole in the ceiling, a squirrel's nest containing blind babies fell out. We were unsure what to do. It became a moral dilemma for us – we literally had life in our hands; we were masters of its fate. The electrician, who was present, told us to throw the squirrel's babies in the nearby stream. Instead, we put the nest in a bucket and left it outside at the spot where we had often seen the squirrel. Within an hour they were gone. I hope the squirrel had rescued its babies, but whatever happened, we let nature take its course. We could never drown the squirrel's babies. When I was a child, I had heard stories of how country folk would drown feral kittens, but I'm glad to say this is an unfounded myth in my experience. Dai Davies was the local farmer, in his seventies, who owned most of the land around the area, and everyone knew him. In his farm lived many cats, all feral. I was at the farmhouse one day when his wife, Miar, was feeding them and around 20 kittens and cats arrived. She fed them twice a day. And she was proud to inform me that they'd never had a problem with mice. The cats were part of the working order of the farm.

It was in spring when the hares came out. Sarah, my neighbour who lived in The Farmhouse, a woman in her early sixties, would often see them early in the morning on her way to work. I had never seen hares before and wondered if I'd be able to tell the difference between a large rabbit and a hare.

'Oh, you'll know straight away that it's a hare!' Sarah said.

'I think I'd be scared of a hare if I saw one; they're aggressive.'

Perplexed, Sarah asked me why I would ever think that a hare could hurt me.

'Well, they're known for boxing.'

Sarah laughed and rolled her eyes.

'They box each other – not people!' She carried on laughing. 'What am I a going to do with you?' She often laughed at my city ways.

Hares usually come out at early dawn and dusk. And in early March, they are known to box frantically with each other. They do this because they are in their mating season, with the males (bucks) seeking out any females (does) that have come into season. The boxing part comes about when the male is too persistent and chases the female. Exasperated, the female will try and fend off the male with a fierce boxing match.

I finally saw a hare one evening, and I knew it was a hare, not a rabbit, straight away. It was bigger with long limbs. It looked far more elegant than a rabbit. The difference between a rabbit and a hare is as that between a pony and a thoroughbred racehorse.

My place had shrunk in the world; I existed in limited places, and this spring, it was the garden that I made my home in. I became the maker of a garden; a seeder; a planter; a giver of water and nature's helping hand. It is a common fallacy to assume that, because you have shrunk your space in the world, you have minimised yourself with it. The world had become more potent; I could feel the pregnant belly of the Earth. You can't help but feel closer to the divine when you're helping the land to flourish. The job of growing produce was an important task. In this area, people would often exchange seeds, seedlings and young plants. The majority of people have polytunnels and grow things all year round. I began to notice things that I had never noticed before; the small changes of nature that I never witnessed in the plumes of smoke of the city. I was no longer just a voyeur of nature: I was a participant.

I expected the pie chart of my life to have fewer segments living in the country. But when you become so engrossed in something so wholeheartedly, it becomes a world of its own; a whole in itself. And you inhabit it with awe and wonder. My world became bigger; I started to notice more. Some of the greatest minds have not lived broadly but deeply. Einstein wore variations of the same grey suit every day so as not to waste brainpower on the trivialities that exist in day-to-day living. Steve Jobs wore blue jeans, a black polo neck and trainers most days. They both chose the worlds they wished to exist in and lived inside them. Choice is often seen as desirable and important, but I was beginning to see how, at times, it might just be a distraction from the greater things in life.

A pair of magpies made a nest in the hawthorn tree close to the house. Every morning they gave a spellbinding dance that circled The Long Barn. The pond that we had put in now had frogspawn in it. Frogspawn attached itself to the edges of the pond and I watched it grow: frogspawn, tadpoles and then frogs. I became a child in a microscopic life. In childhood, it is always spring.

12

IN SPRING THERE IS LIFE

Six years ago, my mother had finished chemotherapy. It was the spring of 2014. You never feel good news so profoundly until all you've heard is bad news for months and months. 'Praise God,' she said. 'Praise God for the good news.' We spread the good news like wildfire to her brother and my cousins and aunts. It felt biblical. I felt all the stories from the Bible, stories of miracles and Easter. I was drunk on good news.

Before the cancer, 'Praise God' was said in high spirits. But since cancer came into our lives, life had become muted, so even 'Praise God' was said in humility rather than exaltation.

An inch of hair had grown back on my mother's head. Looking at her head was like the excitement of seeing the first inch of snow, or the first daffodil of spring or the blossom of a tree. For so long, we had yearned for the newness of beginnings.

It was fitting that it was in spring that she would be in remission – the first growth of hair in unison with the Earth, a springtime symphony. The Earth brought her flowers.

I was never religious like many members of my family. But this spring I felt the breath of God upon my skin. I was humbled by life and the power of prayer. We had all prayed for this day, and our prayers had been answered. I was so thankful that I no longer felt the trouble of what had been. All the bad times of our lives were shadows of the past, and it's futile to dance with shadows. We had too much living to do now. The hurt of the past would stay in the past. A line had been drawn and wouldn't be crossed. That spring we all felt life so profoundly, not just my mother's life, but all our lives. We felt the miracle of life. We had become conscious of the blood that now flowed in our veins like a determined river, breaking riverbanks. That spring our blood overflowed, and in joint communion we drank from the cup of life. And God wiped our tears. '"He will wipe away every tear from their eyes," and there will be no more death or mourning or crying or pain, for the former things have passed away.' (*Berean Standard Bible*, Revelation 21:4)

After the hospital appointment that confirmed no cancer cells were showing, we went to my nan's house where we drank tea and ate samosas. We couldn't go back to the family home because my father and I were no longer speaking. I had confronted him about coming home drunk the day my mum had chemo. His response was to disown me, so he threw me out of the house when my mother needed me the most. I couldn't visit her in our family home, so we had to make other arrangements. But my mother and I didn't fight this with him; we were too busy fighting for her to stay alive. I was incredulous that my father would do this to us; bring more problems, more things for us to fight for. We were already overwhelmed with the numerous hospital appointments; trying to become overnight experts of cancer; trawling the internet trying to find the best ways in which to help my mother. We bought manuka honey, blueberries and pomegranate juice, and visited private doctors and homeopathic clinics. We were exhausted. Unable to handle my mother's diagnosis, my father had turned to drink. And the house became unsafe.

Over the years, my father's drinking had mellowed. When I was a child, his drinking was at its worst. As a grown-up, I saw parts of him that I couldn't see as a child. He was a curious man who wanted to better himself and read books on Gandhi and philosophy. And I loved him for it. The first film he ever took me and my siblings to see in the cinema was *Gandhi*. I was eight years old and became fully aware of the injustices in the world. My father taught me to fight like a warrior against life's injustices – most of which were at my doorstep. I later went on to study politics and philosophy, which made him proud. He would take us to the library as children, and I became a reader of not just books but graffiti on subways and words scribbled on my school desk. Most of all, I became the reader of words that were never allowed to be spoken. But all this goodness was contaminated with alcohol. And the seeds were planted and sown – we became a family that would never have peace. The relationship taught me to forgive. There is a temptation for others to think that, perhaps, this forgiving part of me that can see the goodness in my father is coming from the little girl part of me that wishes to save him. Quite the contrary: it's coming from the worldly woman part of me that has an understanding of the complexities of being human. I understand that stories that don't have happy endings don't necessarily mean there was no happiness along the way. Stories have a beginning, middle and end. We can't leave out the middle part of our lives because we're too devastated by our ends. That wouldn't be the truth – we must tell our stories with veracity and look them in the eye.

Back in the spring of 2014, when my mother was in remission, I could have forgiven anything and I wanted to be with my father. It would have been too cruel to take away the only thing that had been stable, our mother. And just when she had found some joy in her life. She had married at 18 and it was only when she turned 50 that she started to enjoy her life. She had found courage and strength to be who she wanted to be: a woman who loved Christ and people. She flirted with life; joie de vivre had entered her. My father had mellowed in his advancing years and they got on better back then. And my heart had never been so full as it was when I saw them happy and we were a 'normal' family. It's what I had always wanted. We had family holidays and no longer lived in the haunted house of the past, and I no longer envied the functionality of other families. So to take away my mother now, at just 62, in the springtime of her life when she was finally happy and free, would be too much to bear. And so, you see, she had to live. It may seem too everyday to be sitting at my nan's house drinking tea and eating samosas in the presence of such jubilation. But when death threatens your life so imminently, it is the everyday that you want. Nothing makes the ordinary so extraordinary as when death takes a seat beside you.

That spring we celebrated mum's remission in church. It's what she wanted. She stood up in front of the congregation, microphone in hand, and gave her testimony, and gave thanks to God: Praise God. The day of the testimony was the first time I saw my father after he had thrown me out. Knowing he was going to be there filled me with anxiety. But when we both saw each other, we smiled and said hello. He looked like a broken man. It made me feel sad, because all I wanted to do was hug him. I wanted to tell him it was all going to be OK, and that we could all start again. Everything was better now, mum was better and we could all be a family. God had finally smiled on our home.

After the church service, my cousins and uncle and aunt served a celebratory lunch in the church hall. And we were all so happy and full of joy dishing out lamb curry and rice to the fellow worshippers. There was a palpable joyfulness in the air. It was Christmas and Easter: a birth, a near-death and then a resurrection. As we served food, the joys of life fluttered around us like butterflies. All was well in the world. There was no time to waste. We had to live. Live. And live. And then live some more.

SUMMER

13

GOATS AND THEIR HOOVES

The spring slipped into the glory of summer. It was not just the flowers that popped out but the people too. Suddenly the green landscape had a flourishing of colour; wild flowers and villagers with broad smiles. The sun shone on the valley and the surrounding hills, the people, the insects and the little river – all sang in unison.

One fine summer's day, I visited Caer Cadwgan – the nucleus of the valley; a hub of activity. Guests would be staying at the B&B, kids would be playing on their bikes and trampoline and Andy would be looking after the livestock. And the polytunnel would be in its full summer flourish.

'Kiran, we're about to trim Mavis's hooves. Why don't you help? I'll make a countrywoman out of you yet!'

Donna was always trying to turn me into a countrywoman, and I was always a willing apprentice. I would 'do a Jane!' and be a doer in life. I was open to all the new experiences that the countryside had to offer me. It was never my plan to live in the countryside; it was a place I ran to for long weekends, and to actually live here was unthinkable. But I could either be someone who wished things had been different and was back in the city, or I could be a person who immersed themselves in a new way of being and was open to life. I decided I wanted to be the latter. I had always been the latter. I had never trimmed the hooves of a goat before.

After a cup of tea, we made our way to the goats' pen, which was in front of the house. Guests at the B&B liked the goats and children liked to feed them. Donna and I got hold of Mavis, a golden-coloured goat with chocolate-coloured markings on her forehead. The goat didn't want to be held and it was a struggle to keep her still, so Andy came to help. Hoof trimming is an essential part of looking after goats. They need to be checked on a regular basis for hoof growth, as overgrown hooves can make walking painful. Regular goat hoof trimming helps prevent hoof rot, a hoof infection. Wild goats that roam in rocky areas naturally wear down their hooves. On a hot summer's day, I was helping Donna and Andy trim Mavis's hooves. Donna showed me what to do. With something that looked like garden pruners, she cleaned out Mavis's hoof of any stones or anything that was stuck. This took some time, as Mavis wasn't happy to stand still. Then using the pruners, Donna trimmed the hoof. The smell coming from the hoof was foul and it smelt like something rotting, which I didn't expect. I cupped my nose and mouth with my hands, afraid that the smell would make its way into my nose and mouth. But Donna had other plans and handed me the pruners, after showing me, rather expertly, how it was done. The hoof was tough and I struggled with trimming it at first. I was nervous of hurting Mavis; to the untrained eye, the whole process appeared rather brutal. But many things that I thought brutal actually weren't; they were just things that were done in my new environment.

The hooves seemed to be made from the same material as human nails; a kind translucent malleable material. I trimmed away the ragged edges of the inner hoof wall between two halves of the hoof, gingerly. Donna and Andy suggested I trimmed deeper, and shouldn't be so fearful, but I was still afraid that I would hurt Mavis. I had seen how people handled farm animals, with far more force; it wasn't mean or unnecessarily heavy-handed, it was just the way large animals had to be held and navigated. With this in mind, I stopped treating Mavis as though she was a domestic kitten, and held her hoof tight in my grip. It's when you see a clean, white and slightly pinkish sole that you need to stop trimming a goat's hoof. That's when the job is done. Trimming the hooves was a very physical job; trying to hold the goat as it struggled and then removing the debris and finally trimming the hoof. It was a smelly and a tiring job. And this was just one little job at the smallholding. I thought about the other jobs that would have to be done to look after the pigs, the geese, the chickens and the sheep. Most of the jobs I probably didn't even know existed. I always held a naive picture in my head of farming life; a wholesome picture that sat in my head in a warm glow. But I was learning and getting first-hand experience of it, and it was difficult, uncomfortable and exhausting. I felt I was in a position of privilege having had this experience, one that city people pay for when they take their children to farms. Much like bottle-feeding a lamb, which I also had a chance to do. I felt rather elated.

It was one of those days in summer when the sun burnt a hole in the sky, so I wasn't looking forward to my walk back home. The walk from Caer Cadwgan to The Long Barn would take around 45 minutes. I would pass Dai's farmhouse where there is an open barn and you can sometimes see their feral cats sleeping on top of the bales, all stretched out, exhausted by the heat. Opposite the open barn is a country letterbox that I often walk down to to post my letters. Turn left at this crossing and you pass a few picturesque detached houses. It is here that you walk down a very narrow road.

Nothing looks more beautiful in the summer than the Welsh valleys. The valleys become a celebration of the colour green; the hills, in unison, recite an ode to the colour. The season of summer is the season of The Jolly Green Giant, who knocks on the doors of the residents and asks them to come out to play. Here, in the cold months, people shut their doors and the atmosphere is heavy with the sodden blanket of winter. And the existence of people becomes a myth; they turn into ghosts. You will rarely see them, but you may spot one or two as they huddle their way from A to B.

In the summer, when we left our doors and windows open, we were plagued with flies. Especially if the cows had entered the field and the flies came out in full force, attracted to the huge cowpats. Being so close to the field, flies swarmed our house and would then leave their eggs in our cat Truffle's dinner. Truffle had been with us for 15 years.

The whole fly business is one disgusting affair and a reality of living in the middle of the country. Flies also lay their eggs in the woolly coats of the sheep. When there is an accumulation of faeces on a sheep's tail, the flies are attracted to them and lay maggots on the faeces and then in the wool. These maggots will attack the sheep's skin, eventually killing it by literally eating the sheep alive. There are a number of ways to help prevent this dog-eat-dog way of life in the wilds of the country. You can take a pair of shears and remove the maggot-infested wool. Another is to just leave the wool and squirt it with loads of chemical that will kill the maggots. There has been some discussion over which is the best way to help the sheep. If you cut the wool off, resulting in the exposure of the skin that has been chewed away by maggots, the sheep can get sunburn.

In the summer, seeing the sheep run around without their woolly coats made me feel happy, as there would be no maggots eating at their flesh. But flies and maggots were not the only cruelty the sheep had to endure. I had learnt from Dai that certain birds, such as crows, would often pick at the eyes of lambs just as they were being born. This was a regular occurrence in the countryside, and it was something I hoped I would never see. The countryside wasn't a place where nothing happened; it was a place where everything happened. A place where life and death sat beside each other so conspicuously.

I saw a fellow walker and we nodded a hello. Strangers stuck out like neon highlighter pens in the country. I passed the small little bridge with a bejewelled stream. A lady pruned her roses outside her cottage. 'Hello!' she said, clippers in hand and a smile as wide as the horizon.

I passed a few horses running in small fields. They seemed happy. It was summer and I felt every living thing that I had encountered in the countryside smile at me: horses, sheep, lambs, Pygmy goats, Shetland ponies, cows, geese, chickens and alpacas. I realised that it was possible to walk around in all this exuberance and still feel sad, and sadness has a way of making itself known.

My sadness sat on me like a sumo wrestler. My happiness levels only reached so far, an inbuilt barometer of sorts that sometimes made sure only my sadness overflowed. In those melancholic years, the first few years after my mother died, I had never felt life so acutely. And I still felt things so profoundly, and noticed things: the yellow Welsh poppies that grew out of stony old walls, the smells carried by the summer air; I noticed life. I possessed a feeling for beauty and all things that were allowed to be free. I had a new taste for life, not in a 'Let us eat and drink, for tomorrow we die' way, but in a way that was gentle. I was beginning to understand that there was no running away from all the things that had hurt me; the only way out was in. Everywhere I looked I saw the ruins of my life, great cathedrals, with bits of me clinging onto spires, flapping around like old rags.

A sheep trailer passed me. The road is so narrow that you need to hold onto the sides of the stone walls or bushes to avoid being hit by oncoming traffic. I was parched and drank from my water bottle. I was grateful for the passing trailer, as it was an excuse to stop walking; it was getting steeper. The pungent smells from the vehicle awakened all my senses. I wondered whether the sheep were being taken to market, a new field or an abattoir.

14

A DAY AT THE SEASIDE

It was summer 2010, three years before my mother was diagnosed with cancer. My mother and father went to France with me and Simon. They stayed with us in our holiday home, and we all travelled together and would leave together. We were there for four days. My mother and father were getting on and they bantered and chatted about who looked older. Simon and I cooked dinner while my mum and dad went for a stroll around the village. They had been away for a while, and I was worried that they had got lost and was constantly looking out of the window. I heard their voices before I saw them come round the corner. I felt like scolding them for taking their time and making me worry. But I looked at them and felt so happy that I could cry. They were chatting away so much that they forgot the time. I imagined this was the same feeling parents had when they said that all they want is for their children to be happy. I felt the same about my parents. I could forgive the alcohol-soaked years of the past if I saw that the future was rosy. My parents looked as happy as the parents of the children I envied. On that short summer break we visited vineyards, ate in restaurants and Simon and I cooked for my parents. We were a family; not broken, not bruised, not angry, not hurt, not drunk – but functioning. I remember feeling like I was ten years old (I wish it had really been like this when I was ten). We visited a gorge, millions of years in the making, and the gorge tapped into my father's curious and intellectual side, the side of my father that made sense to me. The father that I was proud of.

There would be no other holidays with my family. Those days had ended, and I felt that end like a sledgehammer. So the memories of holidays past lingered around like some golden era. What I had now was a stream of friends who visited us in Wales. People visited us in the summer months: we had become curiosities.

When we had visitors, we would take them to the sea, which wasn't that far away from us. LLangrannog was 23 miles away, a pretty seaside village. Then there was New Quay, a popular harbour 20 miles away, where the writer Dylan Thomas lived during 1944–5, with Aberaeron harbour full of boats and pastel-coloured houses close by. The Cardigan Bay coastline has the largest population of bottlenose dolphins in Europe, and some of the cleanest beaches in the UK, attracting an abundance of marine life. It was here that I saw a sunfish, and was also served the best fish and chips!

When Graham and Sofia, our friends from London, came to stay, we visited LLangrannog – my favourite beach. We laid down a blanket by a huge rock and sat cross-legged. We ate crisps and sandwiches that I made, and looked out towards the sea. We were usually a chatty bunch, but we ate and stared out in silence. This sea would outlast our friendship and anything else that belonged to us. I felt both finitude and infinity simultaneously. I wondered if they were thinking the same, and if not, what it was they were thinking in their silence. Were we all being held together by the same thought?

Sofia removed her clothes and revealed a navy blue swimming costume. She announced, in her Spanish accent, that she was going for a swim. And then Graham took off his shirt – he was already wearing swimming trunks – and said he would join his wife. I stayed where I sat with Simon and we silently watched them frolic in the sea. Sofia carried on going out further until she became a dot of a person. She was half-mermaid, a keen swimmer who felt alive when she swam in the open ocean. She swam with elegance and grace, and for a while, she made the sea her home. I wasn't sure whether it was her swimming skills that made me envious or how she could make a home in both land and sea; she made peace with something so foreign, so alien. I had never swam on the UK shores – they were far too cold, and I wasn't a confident swimmer. I would only go in the sea when I was on a foreign holiday where it was guaranteed to be warmer. And even then I screamed as I entered it, like a baby leaving the warmth of the womb and entering the world.

Sitting on the beach and facing the sea, on the left above the hilltop, an old Victorian white house sat perched on the edge of a cliff. It looked dramatic in any season, especially when the wind was howling. This imposing grand Victorian house, looking to sea, seemed to belong in an old Agatha Christie story; full of romance, charm and drama. Its presence was one of the reasons I liked coming to LLangrannog. At that point, I had no idea about its history, whether it was now a B&B or remained a single residence. I wanted to keep the romance of it alive so that all its details remained a mystery to me.

We walked up the stony steep steps cut into the coastal rock that took us to the cliff path, where we would walk across back to the car. Graham and Sofia talked about their children and plans for the future; how one day they might retire to Spain. The future was laid out in front of them like a well-organised picnic. I had a problem thinking about what lay ahead – I had only existed in the now, and sometimes in the past, for the last six years. It is said that we should all live in the moment more, in the now of our lives. I was beginning to think that this only really happens in deep sadness, when we are so conscious of how we feel at the present time. It's so consuming that we only know how we feel now; we are unable to think ourselves out of the present. The future is talked about when there is hope. The future is always positive simply because we dare to believe that there is one.

We walked to the tip of the cliff, so vast, so eternal. A buttercup-and-daisy-covered terrain. And that afternoon it belonged to us. Brown rabbits popped up everywhere and we all chatted away and drank in the summer. We walked down to the tip of the cliff, where the sea met the earth, and we saw the sea and the earth in one eyeshot. Everything seemed so clear: this was the green of the earth and that was the blue of the sea. Blue and green, the colours of maps, globes and planet Earth from space. We were all sitting on this giant rock that turned on its axis circling the Sun: what a circus. We reached the end of the cliff and stood on its edge, soaked up the sun and tasted the salty breeze. We watched the kayakers and surfers make the sea their playground.

'Can you see that dark shadow there, look!' Simon noticed everything; he had an eagle's eye.

'What are we looking at?' Sofia shouted.

Pods of dolphins were swimming towards us. It was hard to distinguish them from the shapes in the waves and the glare of the sun made it harder to see. But they were there and we could see them. Their dark shadows came closer to us as if with purpose. We felt spoilt; for a very short time the dolphins were here and they were gracing us with their presence. For us, they were masters of the sea, and we were the keepers of the Earth. And even though our hair and jackets were blowing in the wind, for a moment, the Earth stood still in the wind's salty embrace, as we and the dolphins acknowledged our positions in the world. I felt the fragility of life; the spinning of the Earth, a sun that burned too brightly and the eternity of the sea. It made me feel giddy. I loved my friends, yet I couldn't help but wish I was with my mother, sharing this sight, this wonder. I remembered the words on a clock my grandfather had on the wall in the living room for as long as I can remember: 'Welcome all wonders in one sight! Day in Night! And God in Man.' A thought entered my head and came out as a whisper: 'There is no corner of the Earth that I could travel to and not think of you, Mum.'

I hoped the wind would carry my whisper out to sea or that the dolphins would hear it. Some experiences live in our bones.

After the cliff path walk, we did something so normal: we bought ice creams from the kiosk and we took our time dithering about what flavour we wanted. From standing on the cliff and seeing and feeling so much, swallowing the enormity of the Earth, to then debate about which ice cream flavour was best made me feel like I had just travelled back from the moon. The extraordinary wrapped up in the ordinary. I wondered how astronauts felt after seeing the Earth from Space and then coming back to Earth. Would they live any differently now that they had seen the world from a distance?

The four of us licked our ice creams and I was comforted by the sound of our chatter and the familiarity of voices. We were friends, we were alive and we loved each other. People say very good friends are just like family; an elevated position for a friend. But the greatest pain inflicted upon me was from some members of my family. I had never felt such vitriol than from those who had once claimed to love me. I thought of Aristotle's idea of friendship: friends mirrored who we were. No one would choose to live without friends, even if they possessed all the other riches of the Earth.

We left the beach and went straight out to dinner at a pub called The Talbot in Tregaron.

I loved The Talbot because there is a legendary story attached to it. In the summer of 1848, Batty's Travelling Menagerie visited Tregaron as part of its tour of Wales. One of the three elephants belonging to the Victorian circus, named Jwmbi, fell ill and died, and it is said the elephant was then buried behind the pub. A small-scale excavation took place in 2011, but failed to unearth any evidence, though it is still part of an ongoing investigation. The pub celebrates the story of the buried elephant with beer mats featuring the fabled creature and pictures of an elephant on the walls. It helps keep the story alive and is part of the charm of The Talbot. It made me think that perhaps people's lives were just like this elephant's tale; like stories, lives carried on, even after they had ended, just as long as someone kept on telling their story.

15

A WALK ON A SUMMER'S DAY

'London, I hear, is a place best avoided,' Wilf said as I stopped to talk to him.

I was on one of my long walks on what was a perfect summer day. Wilf was in his shed moving stuff and doing farming things.

'So, you've never been to London?' I responded.

He shook his head. 'I think living in a city would be terrible – living on top of one another in great tower blocks and never seeing the sky. I could never do that. That's how it is, isn't it?'

You would think people who lived in tall buildings would be closer to the sky, just as you might think that a person in a church, mosque or temple was closer to God. It was a silly logic; it was possible to be close to something and yet be so far away from it. It was true, the sky was clearer out here in the country – it covered everything, a dome that housed us all. Yes, Wilf, I thought, some people could live in the tallest of skyscrapers and never see the sky.

Wilf was a man of few words, but when he spoke, his words would send me down a spiral of thoughts. And my thoughts would crash into each other, scrambling for attention. I never realised I was so London-centric until Wilf revealed he had never been to my hometown. Only then to discover that he had been outside his valley just once – and that was 30 years ago. What would he think of London? The 'mind the gap' message that rang in the ears of every commuter and the way Londoners closed themselves off in their self-made capsules as they sat on the Tube. For Wilf, my hometown was as foreign as India.

'Many of my friends I grew up with left to find work in the big cities,' he continued, chatting while he tore open the feed for his sheep. 'As a young man, I was offered a job in Scotland on the oil rigs, but I could never leave.'

I imagined next would come a tale of an ailing mother or father who forced him to forget his dreams for the sake of the family's farm. A tale of sacrifice and dreams that a young man was no longer allowed to have.

'My heart belongs here with the birds and the trees. I knew, if I left, I'd be thinking about my valley the whole time, so what would be the point? All I want is right here.'

And in those few spoken words, casually uttered, and to some so easily forgotten, Wilf became the richest man I'd ever known. He started to cry; he felt his words deeply, and was moved by his own life, as someone might be moved by seeing a Rembrandt or a Picasso. As always with Wilf, I had never wanted to hold his hand or give him a hug when he got emotional.

I wanted him to be free, never wanting to move forward and crowd him or get in the way of his words. Words were like tsunamis: they could kill you.

'I have never wanted to run away from this life, even as a young lad,' he continued, as he sat down on an old steel drum. I wondered if anyone had ever asked him about his life before while he sat in front of me revealing parts of his life, like glints of sun on a gently running stream. I felt like a child asking questions about life to a grown-up as they worked, and perhaps getting in the way. I half-expected him to ask me to run off and play outside so that he get on with his day. But I had always been a child in life. I had always lived in a constant state of questioning, examination, curiosity and unravelling. But now, I had been reborn, borne out of a dark experience that brewed inside me. I was a child again. And the world was new.

I tried not to see Wilf as a relic from the past, as I stood looking at him sat on the old steel drum, wiping his tears. Besides, he existed now in the present. And there was me running to places far and wide, New York and London, like a magpie to all that was shiny and new. All the while, Wilf stood still. I wondered whether Wilf gawped at me as much as I felt I was gawping at him. And perhaps it's OK to gawp, to recognise difference with reverence and curiosity.

What did he think of me? An Indian woman, unusual in these parts, full of questions and bumbling like a bee? A flibbertigibbet in a Little Red Riding Hood raincoat, with a reckless habit of stepping out onto life's busiest roads?

I wondered if my words stayed with him as much as his stayed with me. This was the way people lingered through our lives, in fragments of sentences that, years later while doing something ordinary like sitting on a bus, we would remember. We would be reintroduced to a lost conversation that suddenly, or had always, made sense to us.

Wilf stood up, 'Look at me, I could never stay indoors and watch TV!'

He was almost shouting now, a protest against living in the city, as if I was threatening to box him up and ship him down to London.

'No, I can't imagine you living that kind of life, Wilf.'

I imagined Wilf inside a house, doors shut, with the world locked out. I had never seen Wilf's house; he lived away from the village. I couldn't imagine him in a home surrounded by domesticity. I had invited him to The Long Barn, but he never accepted any invites, so I had never seen him in an ordinary domestic setting. I imagined that seeing Wilf in a house would be like when I was a kid and I saw my schoolteacher out shopping on a Saturday morning: it didn't make sense, it was incongruous. As a kid, teachers only existed in school settings. Wilf couldn't exist indoors – not when there was the great outdoors. If Wilf lived in the city with a city job, he would have been retired by now. But he was a 72-year-old farmer who was still working because farming wasn't his job, it was his life. He walked towards his tool cabinet where the tools were meticulously placed; everything was so ordered.

'Walking around my farm fills me with wonder. What makes my life is working outside, only going in if the weather is very bad.'

Wilf was so much part of the outside world, and yet so much apart from it. It is said that the world is our oyster; it's ours for the taking, a place to roam and conquer, and attempt to reign over. This is what the world tells us. But the world was not so much of an oyster for Wilf but a place to nestle in. He had no desire to claim the world, to possess it in any way or even make his mark on it; the world was not his to own. Perhaps it's a natural instinct to want to leave our mark; it's something that I had once understood well. But I no longer had that notion. I no longer wanted to conquer the world; the world had conquered me and I had much to ruminate.

'Well, it's a lovely day today,' I said gaily.

It was an almost-nothing thing for me to say in the face of what had just been said. But I didn't know what to say; I had become an almost silent observer of things. It was the outside that was alive; inside I was dead. I had nothing to offer. But Wilf heard my bland comment and replied: 'The best.'

Wilf started to get busy again, this time with tools and gadgets. It was time for me to leave. Even though he never made me feel unwelcome, I sometimes felt I was holding up a busy farmer who was happily going about his day; the city encroaching on the countryside. I was beginning to worry that my conversations with him opened up some locked-up thoughts and feelings because he cried at most of our exchanges. But for me, our conversations were innocuous and fragranced with childhood innocence; two people who were at odds with the world telling stories of worlds that existed outside their own. Perhaps he cried because no one had asked him to tell his story before? And perhaps I asked him so many questions because I no longer wanted to live in my own story?

I had one last question.

'Wilf, I've stopped hearing the cuckoo. Has it already left for Africa?'

It had just occurred to me that I had not heard the cuckoo for a while. I was unsure whether it had left or I had become so used to it that I had stopped hearing it, even though it was still present.

Wilf raised his head and with glittering eyes said:

> 'In April I open my bill
> In May I sing all day
> In June I change my tune
> In July away I fly
> In August fly away I must'

The cuckoo had left. We both smiled with a slight giggle, acknowledging the sweetness of the rhyme and the bittersweetness of life. And with that I bid Wilf farewell and carried on with my walk.

I walked up the road, just before the Roman road crossing, and watched freshly shorn sheep run in the fields. The price of wool was almost next to nothing, Wilf had told me: 15–37p per kilogram. It cost more to get someone to shear the sheep. So sheep were shorn not for any profit from wool but for the sake of the sheep; it kept them cool in the summer, and with no woolly coats, there could be no maggot infestation. With farmers selling sheep fleeces at rock-bottom prices, I couldn't understand why a 100-per-cent wool jumper would then cost a great deal of money in the shops.

I passed fields ablaze with green and viewed the rawness of the countryside. Things didn't hide themselves here; they were either present or not. After all the excitement of the arrival of the cuckoo back in spring, after much fanfare, it had left unnoticed. No one mentioned that the cuckoo no longer sang, and there was no sadness at its departure, certainly no feelings that matched its arrival. Things came and went so easily here. It was an accepted brutal fact of life that things came and went; life had a rhythm that it must adhere to. In this way, the countryside simplified life in the understanding that there was a time to live and a time to die.

I thought about Wilf's tears; the country air softened life, a watercolour of a painting. And when it rained, which it often did in Wales, it was a Monet. The philosopher Seneca said: 'What need is there to weep over parts of life? The whole of it calls for tears.' This was Wilf. And in the last few years it was me. Life made me cry in both its beauty and its sadness. I was beginning to think that beauty was often laced with sadness, that it couldn't exist in the vacuum of its own glory. It was what the Japanese called *mono no aware*, the bittersweet realisation of the ephemeral nature of all things, the awareness that everything in existence is temporary. The fleetingness of the seasons is not to be mourned but cherished, their impermanence appreciated, for that is where their beauty comes from. Wilf was not crying because he was sad, he was crying because life was beautiful.

A few lambs had escaped their fields and blocked the road that I was walking down. I tried to hurry them along by walking faster, hoping that they would have the sense to part and walk to the side, but they didn't. They just hurried faster in front of me, moving further away from where they had come from. They were silly little things. They kept looking back to see if I, the bogeyman, was still following them, which I was of course. Then one of the three lambs launched itself into a hedge on the side of the road and clambered onto the top of the hedge. And for a few moments it was King of the Valley, viewing life from above. The two other lambs followed suit, but weren't as skilful as the first one and made a pig's ear out of their great escape; funny creatures. I stopped and watched, and almost cheered out loud when they too made it to the top of the hedge. Escaped lambs on country roads were a common occurrence; an annoyance for many. The traffic here was so different to the traffic in London. But I didn't mind. I enjoyed watching new life explore and wander. Only the curious get lost and feel the joys of finding and being found.

My younger self would have never understood Wilf and how his curiosity didn't implore him to explore outside his valley. We would never have found each other. I would have asked: what can you learn from standing still? The philosopher Immanuel Kant lived his entire life in Königsberg and barely travelled outside the city. He would wake up at 5am every day, he'd have lunch in the same restaurant at the same time every day and he'd go for a walk in the same park on the same route every day. Perhaps a myopic existence for many, but a life no less full. I was beginning to appreciate lives lived like this. I began to understand the beauty of a microscopic life.

The thing with life is that it's not stagnant; we give meaning to whatever we choose to assign meaning to. It was freeing to know this. Because of Wilf, I was beginning to understand that there was movement in standing still – if you noticed the seasons so acutely and if you allowed yourself to listen to the cuckoo. He was rooted like a tree, his roots running deep into the earth of his valley. I had never wanted to be a tree in life. But now I longed to be rooted more than anything. I wanted to be like Wilf. I wanted roots to press into the concrete road I was walking on and then push deeper and deeper down until they reached the core of planet Earth. I needed the soles of my feet to feel the magnetic pull of the Earth, to not let me roam any further. I wanted my freedom to be taken away; I was longing to be still. I never thought one could feel so imprisoned within one's own freedom. And I never thought being rooted could feel so much like belonging.

On the bend of the road, a man with a dog passed me and we both nodded a greeting and smiled under a beaming sun. I had never seen this person before, I thought. And then I laughed at myself. I had become quite the countrywoman; I noticed strangers and thought, 'They're not from around here.'

A summer breeze passed through me, as if I were a ghost. I could feel my own hollowness; a ghost passing through a world of green. Wilf said he was surrounded by all that he desired: the birds and the trees. I was envious of him, a man who was content with so little. But I wasn't sure nature could be described as a 'small' or 'little' pleasure. Nature was everything; even when I was living in London and divorced from it, it had still been everything. Wilf wasn't content with so little; he was content because he had so much. There was a time when I would have seen contentment like Wilf's as the poor relation to happiness. Happiness in its exuberance swings from chandeliers, whereas contentment enters our lives quietly. I had always thought that to find oneself, one must travel far and wide. It was an anomaly that someone could find themselves where they already stood. Not everyone wanted to run away in life. I was beginning to learn that some people were happy just where they found themselves. Unlike me, they didn't have to press every button that life presented only then to find some more. But still, it was OK to be me, to waltz life's perpetual revolving door. I had an innate curiosity that made me want to see things from the other side.

I had often been accused of being 'easily pleased' because of my enjoyment of simple things: a favourite book from my childhood or watching dogs frolic by the sea. In a world where we are all striving to be happy and content, 'easily pleased' should surely be a goal? The probability of being happy for someone who's easily pleased is far greater than someone who's not. As I carried on with my walk and felt the sun on my face, I realised 'easily pleased' was actually a superpower. And it belonged to Wilf and had once belonged to me. There seems to be a belief that anything worth having takes a lot of striving; that the road to happiness needs to be fraught with difficulties. My younger self would have asked him to get out of the valley and see more, be more. But why? Why was the contentment and happiness he felt questioned as if it were not enough or even real? Perhaps we all had an insatiable want for happiness, a thirst that was never quenched? And so, when we met someone who was content and happy, we never quite believed them. In our search for it, we had all made happiness and contentment a mythical state of being.

I passed a stream and stopped to listen to it. I always made time to stop and see or hear anything that gave me some joy. It had become part of my survival. The smell of sunshine filled my nostrils. I crouched down to be closer to the stream and drank in its smell. I stretched out so that my hot sticky fingers could feel its trickle. Soft Welsh water flowed through my fingers feeling like silk. I splashed my face with the water; a mini baptism. I was alive – only people who were alive could feel dead. I sat down on the ground and crossed my legs. And listened. My favourite piece of music, 'The Lark Ascending', filled my head like an old prayer that someone had once whispered for me. I could hear it so clearly; it held my face in its hands, demanding that I heard it. It joined the rest of the mellifluous sounds of summer in a symphony that wrapped around me; a fragile chain of musical notes. I felt the touch of hundreds of people as they placed their hands upon me. And they were the hands of all the people I had ever known, everyone who cared or had once cared for me. They passed me through from one person to the next, their hands stretched above their heads as I surfed a sea of people: old schoolteachers, friends, dead people that I loved. I was cushioned by them, protected by the prayer and wrapped around by the heavy weight of a summer breeze. I was being carried. I had been tired for so long. I started to sob by the stream, overwhelmed by the prayer, summer, hearing 'The Lark Ascending', being carried by the sea of people and by life. I was overwhelmed by it all. My chest heaved as my heart overflowed and a waterfall of tears made itself known. I was alive. I felt everything.

16

THE CRIES OF THE LAMBS

The next day, after my long walk and chat with Wilf, there was a disconcerting sound in the valley. And then I remembered what Wilf had told me, that in the summer the ewes were separated from their lambs. And all around the valley, the cries of the lambs and the ewes weighed heavy in the air; the high-pitch sound of the lambs and the guttural sound of the ewes. It was a strange sort of mix, the happiness and exuberance that summer brought, punctuated by the sad sound of lambs leaving their mothers.

The process of separating the ewes from the lambs is known as weaning, and is a means of controlling the lambs' milk intake. The lambs are weaned from a diet that only or mostly consists of milk and introduced to solid feed and grain. It's considered an important part of rearing sheep. As harsh as separating the lambs from their mothers may sound, I expect this was some relief to the ewes. So often, sat on my balcony, I could see lambs that were really quite large suckle at their mothers forcefully.

You could tell that the mothers by this stage were rather tired from feeding their lambs and tried to kick and shake the lambs off them.

The separation process is also a way for farmers to control costs, as lactating ewes with feeding lambs require more feed. The ewes are removed from the pen and placed in a separate one away from the lambs. For the process to be less stressful, the lambs are often placed in groups of siblings. Knowing this gave me some comfort, even though it was a comfort that evaded my own life.

The great fallout with my siblings meant I had no way to share memories with the nuclear family that I spent my formative years with. There are stories and incidents that I can only share with my siblings. There are memories of happy days of going to a theme park in the long summer school holidays and just ordinary memories of everyday living. We were all so different, so we never really gelled, but sometimes we partially did. I'd be lying if I said that the absence of the people who hold the title of brother or sister didn't make me feel lonely or somehow a little ill-equipped in the world. I felt vulnerable without my own clan; there is safety in numbers. I felt as if everything outside myself was free to pierce me – there was no barrier between myself and it. I was not so much of a lone wolf as a lost lamb. But I had to remind myself that what I missed was having siblings who expressed care and kinship – and this was not them.

What gives me anxiety is that there is no one to correct a memory for me now, no one to say, 'Remember when Mum did/

said . . .' I am alone with my nebulous thoughts. No one will know or remember any childhood memory I have growing up in our family of five. What happens to memories when they cannot be shared? Old photos that document that a family of five did once exist, and sometimes was happy, are around but are not in my possession. They are with my sibling. I am not sure how one navigates their way through life with no one to share memories with and no physical documentation to keep those memories alive. It's something I have yet to find out. One day, in the future, I will wonder if the history that I am certain of now actually really happened. And there will be no one for me to ask. I always believed: 'No man is an island'. Until I became the island.

I would never have thought I'd feel so much affinity with listening to the sound of the lambs being separated from their mothers and possibly their siblings. I almost couldn't bear to hear their cries because I understand them too well.

My neighbour, Sarah, also couldn't bear the sound of the crying ewes and lambs, and at this time of year she walked around with a heaviness in her heart. She would say, 'Those poor lambs.' When she was in The Long Barn, while talking to me, she would be looking out through the large windows and watch the lambs gallop and dance in their fields. It brought her great joy. I loved how her sensitivity for all things that were alive was always on full display. Surrounded by lambs, she was unable to eat them. And should I be cooking or eating lamb, she would make herself scarce. On her way to work, Sarah would pass an abattoir, and because of this, she worked out another route that took her through the mountains, just so that she could avoid the slaughterhouse. This added 30 minutes to her already long journey. She said that every time she saw trailers full of sheep making their way to the abattoir, her heart would break a little for the 'poor darlings'.

One cold, rainy and wintery day, just back from work, she popped into The Long Barn. Her sodden blonde hair stuck to her face and mascara ran down her cheeks. Her smart work clothes were drenched and muddy. I thought she had fallen into a ditch.

She had been driving back from work when she had spotted a sheep on its back, and with a coat heavy with rain, it was unable to get up. Sarah saw the distressed sheep, stopped her car and jumped over the barbed-wire fence, tearing her tights and catching her skirt in the fence. In heels, she ran across the field and pulled the sheep upright, which would have been no easy task. She saved the sheep's life.

Sheep do not lie on their backs naturally, and if they are on their backs, they will be unable to get upright and will die from suffocation. Not just that, they will become vulnerable to being attacked by crows and other animals. Sheep falling on their backs didn't just happen in winter when coats were heavy but during lambing season too. The extra weight carried by pregnant sheep makes them more prone to falling over. Cutting through the mountains on her way to and from work, Sarah would occasionally see sheep on their backs, and she would always save them. Which meant that she was sometimes late for work or late coming back home, and I loved her for it.

When I first heard the crying of the lambs, followed by the cries from their mothers, I felt the whole world crying. It was a sound that deep down, whether we lived in the countryside or not, we would all recognise: the sound of displacement, separation and fear. It was a sound that, in the end, would belong to us all.

17

THE SUMMER PARTY

Later that summer, Caer Cadwgan held a summer party and the community came together. It was a display of joined-up thinking, feverish excitement and palpable anticipation. Leaflets advertising the party were delivered to all the residents. I liked how in the countryside a simple party could become the centre of so much fuss, focus, attention and joy. But what was really surprising was how much pride came with it, not just from the ones who were hosting it, Donna and Andy, but from the whole community.

Running up to the party, familiar faces that I came across while out walking or at the supermarket would excitedly ask: 'Are you going to the big do at Caer Cadwgan?' One morning while driving to town, I passed the local postman, Phil. He stopped his red van, wound down the window and gathered up the post for The Long Barn, handing it through his window. 'Will I be seeing you at the party, then?' He didn't need to specify; I knew the party he was referring to. For a while, it was the talk of the village; it was all that existed. In the city, so many things passed me by, as if the abundance of city parties diluted them, making them insipid and so everyday.

The day before the party, all the people who entered the scarecrow competition had their hard work judged. Andy drove through the village taking photos and made notes of the scarecrows that were standing in people's drives and front gardens. Sarah had spent many evenings after work making her scarecrow. And every so often she would ask for random items, such as chicken wire and the base of a Christmas tree. She was rather secretive about her creation, a sign of her vulnerability; she was a sensitive soul. She would pop in to collect the bits she had asked for, saying: 'Oh, I'm not sure about the scarecrow. It looks a bit hideous. The face is too small.' I rather enjoyed this chatter; few times in our adult lives do we pay that much attention to our creativity, unless we're professional artists. Sarah displayed all the seriousness that a child has for something they have made. It was joyful; there was a beauty in the serious business of getting a scarecrow just right.

On the eve of the party, Sarah wheeled her scarecrow out in front of the drive for us all to see. Our neighbours Glen and Rod and Simon and I all stood outside, even the dogs – Sarah had Daisy and Charlie, and Glen and Rod had three English Setters. We all came out to see the big reveal. The scarecrow wore Sarah's old wedding dress and a handmade crown. It had a cloak made of red velvet that Sarah said was part of the 'going away' outfit her mother wore when she got married. And when she wheeled it out, we all clapped and all the dogs barked. We all felt rather proud. It was magnificent. There was something quite beautiful about all the components that made up the scarecrow; significant parts of Sarah's life. It accentuated the seriousness that she took in the task of building it.

'Well done, Sarah,' Glen shouted across. 'You've made us all look boring for not taking part!' The three English Setters placed their giant paws on the fence and barked at the scarecrow. Although it was Sarah who made it, it became our scarecrow, belonging to Blaenau Isaf. It was a feeling that was dipped in innocence, harking back to a childhood feeling before money and the pressure to be someone ruined us all. Except, perhaps, for Wilf.

With a few local friends, I helped with the day's activities for the summer party. We all arrived four hours early. Together with Andrew's mother Wendy, we had a conveyor belt going. We buttered the bread and filled the sandwiches with either ham, cheese or egg mayo, then Wendy's adult granddaughter cut the sandwiches and placed them in small brown paper bags along with a piece of fruit, crisps and a drink. These brown bags would be placed on a small table at the front of the drive where people could purchase the 'meal deal' bags. The idea was for the summer party to pay for itself – it just needed to cover costs. Donna and Andy were not interested in profits; they were throwing a party for the community. A few other locals arrived and got on with the chores that needed doing. We swept the kitchen floor and laid out tables, while Donna got the 'tuck shop' ready with an array of sweets all placed in old-fashioned sweet jars. She had baked lemon drizzle, chocolate cake and Victoria sponges for afternoon tea.

We were like bees, the community our hive, working together for the greater good. The day sailed through with all the helpers sharing a concern for it to go smoothly. We all had our parts to play and no one was made to feel redundant. Everyone was working in unison; we were equal parts of a whole.

Prizes were given to the best scarecrow, for the furthest welly thrown in the 'welly wanging' competition and the best soapbox racing car. The soapbox race was taken with more seriousness than I would have ever thought possible. Down the hill of Caer Cadwgan the little capsules raced. When Andrew unveiled his racing car, there was genuine astonishment at his creation. While everyone else's cars were rather traditional, his was a thing of envy, even for me. The body of the car was an old battered orange kayak. There was a wheel that looked like a bicycle wheel at the front and then two wheels on either side of it. It had a little rocket with sparks flying out at its tail end when it took off. It was genius. Adding to the whole eccentricity of it all, Andrew wore an old-fashioned leather helmet and goggles you see fighter pilots wearing in old films. He looked magnificent. Although in his fifties, he always had a boyish charm about him and now, standing by his soapbox and wearing a smile as wide as the valley, it was amplified even further.

'I'm going to win this race!' Andrew screamed as he rode down the hill with Andy and a few others. Everyone clapped and kids waved their sticky sweet fingers in the air, holding up the inflatable toys they had won at the pick-a-duck game. The buzz in the air lifted everyone.

Throughout the day, kids rushed around swapping sweets and trying their hand at various games while the adults chatted to one another as they drank tea and ate sandwiches. In the evening, a local covers band would come to play; they required no payment because this was for the community. There would be a barbecue that was manned by local friends, and Andy would man the pop-up pub in one of the sheds, with everyone sat around on bales. Everybody had a stake in the party and it didn't involve money. There was only one goal and that was for everyone to have a good time. It was in the pursuit of the noble and the wholesome.

It was my turn to look after the pick-a-duck game. If you managed to fish out a duck with a red mark at the bottom, you won an inflatable toy. If you didn't 'win', you got a cone full of sweets. The kids were no longer interested in the pick-a-duck and ran around the fields high on sugar. So I sat down and soaked up the day and looked out towards the valley. Dark clouds headed towards us. With all the seriousness of the past years, I meandered around in life heavy-footed, reluctantly anchored to an ill-matched world. The frivolity of scarecrows and soapboxes made me feel light again. Here I was, a brown city girl, in the midst of a big summer party in the countryside with people who didn't look like me, and surrounded by children when I had none of my own. And yet I felt content. I was content in what once I would have considered the unlikeliest of communities for me. In the midst of the things I thought would never fit me, I would have been a meteorite, fallen from something as foreign as the moon. But the moon is not so foreign, not really, not if you took the time to gaze at it.

'Hello!' It was Hara, shouting across to me; she had just arrived. Hara was a sound healer and a woman tied to Mother Earth. She made up chants and released people from any spiritual blockages. She danced, she sang and she swore like a sailor. I loved her. She always wore colourful clothes, but most of all, she wore purple. And as she frantically waved at me as she made a beeline for me, her purple hair was like a beacon of positivity against the brooding dark clouds. She wore fresh flowers in her hair.

'Hey, how are you?' she asked as she sat down beside me on the low concrete wall. Before I could answer, she said: 'It's Si's birthday and I'm making him a mint chocolate ganache cake with a chocolate biscuit base, and then I'm going to bring some over for you!' Hara's husband was also called Simon, though she affectionately called him Si. I laughed because Hara and I always talked about food. 'Aw, thank you, Hara! That sounds bloody delicious!'

Hara always launched into conversation as if there wasn't enough time in the day for all the words that needed to be spoken. So she said everything, all at once.

She asked if I'd tried the pick-a-duck as she got up and had a go herself. I had been watching people all day try and fish for the ducks. I enjoyed watching the look of concentration on their faces, especially the kids. It sounds silly, but I was almost envious of it; this focusing in on something so much that, temporarily, everything else was muted. It was a lesson in living in the moment – and living it well. It was something I was learning to do.

'Hara, I'm so happy you're here.' I said. She was one of those people that made you feel you were allowed to make such declarations without it being awkward or weird. It gave our friendship freedom.

Hara sat herself back down and smiled broadly at me before she said: 'Me too! I've never known anyone to talk about food more than me.'

She had a soft Liverpudlian accent that made everything she said sound extra comforting. She had moved to the valley 30 years ago to live self-sufficiently. She had twin 30-year-old sons who lived away. I had never eaten dairy-free and gluten-free desserts before, but since I met Hara, who lived a 15-minute walk away from The Long Barn, she had introduced me to her dairy- and gluten-free world. Occasionally she would drop off her latest creations – she never used recipes – and tested them out on me. Hara wasn't the type of person to use recipes. I couldn't imagine her using anything that was well established. She made her own rules; to her, life was a blank canvas and she was an artist who enjoyed scatter painting.

'Next time, Kiran, when I come over, I'll make some of my absolute best coleslaw to go with your tandoori chicken, and I'll bring some wine too.' When we talked about food, we talked as though we were plotting some great scheme. 'That would be lovely!' I said.

I offered to make a dessert, but Hara shook her head frantically. 'No, no, no, I have a brilliant idea for a new dessert. You're going to love it!'

I always felt anything was possible with Hara. I felt safe with her. She was a woman in her fifties, but she seemed like a woman without an age to me. She existed without a time frame. And odd as this may sound, the first few times that I had met her, I thought to myself, 'If I die tomorrow, I'd like her to be by my side.' She had an otherworldliness to her that made her appear that she was comfortable with things perhaps others wouldn't be comfortable with. She was open to life in such a radical way that I couldn't imagine anything in life would phase her.

She offered me a glass of wine, but I said no. Daytime drinking never suited me. 'You go ahead,' I said.

She came back 15 minutes later, and even before she had reached me, she was telling me about the conversations she just had at the bar. There are few people in life who can make you feel ageless; people usually make you feel young or old, or the age that you are. And we relate to them accordingly. But with Hara, I forgot myself in a way that I seldom did. I could have been any age. We were both effervescent when we spoke about things that mattered to us, as if we were children. And we knew enough about life to know not to be flippant with it. Hara's mother died at the age of 47, and she spoke openly about it.

Our friendship was a bubble that encased everything that a person could be. How the mind could flutter between chocolate ganache and death. I had always been accused of being 'random' in conversation – I swapped subject matters in a way that was jarring for some. I could laugh and cry in a single conversation. In Hara, I found someone like me. People know that we can be all things at once, but not many people allow it – it's too disconcerting. But Hara knew that to live, to live well, it was important to be free to explore the whole interior of our minds. Both death and chocolate ganache existed – and depending upon what day it was, one was more important than the other.

18

BELONGING AND OTHERNESS

In the late evening of the party, I went home and sat on the balcony of The Long Barn and looked out into the darkness. An evening chill wrapped itself around me. Dark shadows of trees swayed and bats flew close by. The sound of animals and insects surrounded me. But in the distance, the sound of the party and the covers band, which was still in full swing, was swept up by the wind and delivered to me like an unexpected gift. Once, this would have been the sound of familiarity: parties, laughter and music. But now, I wasn't quite sure what was more familiar to me: the sound of the natural world or the exuberance of people. Perhaps we're surrounded by everything simultaneously, but you only notice the things that your heart and soul need.

In the darkness, Caer Cadwgan lit up like a beacon, the sound of the party rolled down to the lower parts of the valley like happy, friendly tumbleweed. It was the valley's very own nucleus; it gave light and energy to everything else. It made me think of Athens and the Parthenon, the temple dedicated to the goddess Athena, high up on the Acropolis. And how, one late evening while holidaying in Greece, I sat in a cafe and stared at the temple lit up in all its glory, accompanied by a full moon. It stood proud in full display as if it was held up by the hand of the goddess herself. And down below, the citizens of Athens, like industrious ants, went about their daily business. Restaurants fed hungry tourists and everyone drank retsina. And this whole endeavour of living and being encircled the Acropolis, with the Parthenon looking down on all the human activities, giving energy to it. Today, Caer Cadwgan, was our very own Parthenon.

Simon gave me a shawl to cover my shoulders, handed me a glass of wine and sat down beside me. We didn't face each other but stared out to the hills and allowed ourselves to be swallowed by the vastness of it all. There was no point being here, away from London, if we weren't prepared to give some part of ourselves up to nature and the simple act of being still. It was Simon who held my hand in all the darkness that followed my mother's death. He didn't try and crowd the path that I had to walk or try and redirect it. I think that's the most loving thing someone can do for you when your life falls apart. To allow you to go through your transformation with little interference, but be on the periphery, within eyeshot, so that you know someone is there, waiting for you, when you are ready to live again.

'It's strange that you can find yourself fitting in things you wouldn't think you'd ever fit,' I said. I wasn't looking for a response; it was just a thought, said out loud into the open air. Sometimes I felt I needed to do this, to empty the thoughts that ran restlessly in my head. And the amphitheatre of the valley that I looked out onto made me feel that perhaps my emptied-out thoughts had some place to roam to find out the things that I could only contemplate.

'Life isn't stagnant; things change, life changes, so we change,' Simon said. He made everything sound so obvious. What he said made me think that perhaps I never really wanted to belong to one place in life. Perhaps to totally fit into one time and one place would mean the end to one's evolution; a full stop. And I never would want to reach a full stop in life.

'So, what's your ideal community?' Simon challenged my thoughts.

'With people who look like me, from the same ancestry, sharing blood and history?' I said, even though I already knew this wasn't true. I wasn't even sure why I said it. Perhaps it was something that someone once told me in my childhood: the only people who will ever understand you and look out for you are your family.

When I visited a village in India in 2016, a place of my heritage and where my relatives live, the women there were fascinated by the fact that I didn't have children. I went on the trip to India with an aunt of mine, who lives in the UK, for a family wedding, and it was a few years after my mother died. I stupidly thought I could find some affinity with the people that were related to me and from the country of my parents' birth. I felt so disconnected since my mother died, I yearned to connect with others who knew my mother. The women couldn't work out what I did with my time if I had no children to care for. Or how I coped with a house that screamed with silence, not with children. They couldn't understand what my reason was for working and earning if I didn't have children to earn for. An aunt asked me: 'What are you doing all this for, all this working and having a lovely home, if you don't have children?' It didn't occur to them that we could do things for their own sake or for the sake of ourselves.

It was as if my life had no value unless it gave life to others. The idea of a non-sacrificial woman was something they had never heard of. There was a freedom that belonged me, as a child-free woman, that they were scratching their heads about. Another aunt suggested I must have a healthy bank balance because I didn't have children. These remarks were essentially comments on my freedom – the freedom to do and the freedom to be. I tried to understand their provincial mentality. Life for them was formulaic: get married, have children and then look after husband, children and home. There was no diverting from this. If that's all there was to do, I had nothing to do.

In the week that I was in India, people offered me potions and all sorts of concoctions and advice so that I could get pregnant, even though I said wasn't interested. I had never made a conscious decision not to have children – it just didn't happen, and that was OK with me. To them, at first, I was a puzzle to be marvelled at, and then a conundrum to be conquered. By the end of the trip to my relatives' village in India, I vowed never to return. I may as well have had two heads, I was that much of a pariah. It was ironic that I went to India to connect with family when the reality was that we were foreigners to one another. I was a girl who was born in the UK and had funny ideas.

Throughout my life, I had become well acquainted with the feeling of 'other'; a separateness and divide from both my culture and my family. Sacred institutions that most people hold dear, family and religion, became objects of suspicion for me when I was growing up, reaching a crescendo when my mother died. My family, a religious family (my grandfather was a pastor), had always been so dysfunctional; fraught with anger and judgement. And as a child, I questioned where God was in all this. Family members, happy and doing well, would always thank God for their blessings. I wondered why God didn't live in my house. And then there was the emphasis and value placed on family. Although so many times we were happy, there was always an underlining and disconcerting hum of fear and unhappiness that vibrated under our feet. It would become the soundtrack of my life, this incoherent dissonance.

But then I found myself in an unusual position: my mother, the keeper of the peace, was dead. The family that I grew up with, my first and most important social group, was gone in a single swoop, as if they had been involved in a horrific car crash. I was now a woman with no foundation. And more than any other time in my life, the world felt overwhelming.

When my mother died, my immediate family could not hold itself together. As much as I tried to keep the stitching of my family intact, they unravelled, as badly stitched things do.

My mother had propped the family up, and when she died, she set us adrift. And we all drowned.

My thoughts went back to Simon's question: what is the ideal community. 'Places that we belong to should make us feel our greater sense of self, a reinforcement of who we are, shared values. Mine just hasn't come from my family, apart from my mother.'

Simon didn't respond; he just listened. Our conversation was a sequence of rambling thoughts that left our hearts and minds and fluttered out into the open space. I imagined our thoughts dangling from the trees, the garden fence and the stars. 'But that can't be true either,' I continued. I knew I didn't share the same politics as many of the people that I had met here, and I could feel our difference. What we did share, though, was a love for community, nature and creativity. 'It's kindness. An acceptance of who I am. A pressure not to be anything else. That's what I've found here.'

And even saying that out loud seemed strange; this small, Welsh, white community could be so accepting of me as I was. In London, I was an integral part of the multicoloured patchwork of the city. In the countryside, there was the odd Indian and Chinese restaurant in the towns, but if I wanted Mexican or Japanese food, I'd have to make it myself. There is little demand for the foreign and the 'exotic'. And in a way, I interpreted that as something the countryside felt about me: not interested in anything foreign. Maybe, if someone is so different from you in background and ethnicity, you expect everything to be different – difference is expected and accepted. But within my own culture and members of my family, because I was like them in so many ways, sharing blood and history, my nonconformity was harder to accept. It was seen as rebellious.

I thought about the party, Hara and Donna and all the children who were allowed to run free. We all existed as we were. 'I guess we all find a place in life, from our favourite position on the sofa to our latest new friend.' And as my words hit the air, I understood it was OK to be a wanderer in life; it didn't mean I was lost or less than. I looked towards Caer Cadwgan, where yellow beads of light streamed down the hill like hot lava; people were leaving the party. Even though I had left the party, I felt sad watching it end; people leaving, the music stopping and watching the lights switch off. I was a distant voyeur to it now. Buddhists say that the root of suffering is attachment. I had never been good at letting things go; I felt the end of things so viscerally. I wish I didn't feel things so deeply.

The day had ended. The last light was switched off. And I tried to remember that there can be no new beginnings without a few ends.

19

THE BIRD OF PREY WHO CAME TO TEA

It was one of those thick, hazy days at the end of summer. Rod, my next door neighbour who lived in The Barn, had been pottering in his garden when he noticed a bird lying in Dai's field. After an hour, he noticed the bird was still there. He popped into The Long Barn to let us know.

'Has anyone else noticed that bird of prey out in the field?' Rod said as he entered the house. In the heat and sunlight, everything seemed to be fully alive, so to hear that something might only be partially alive felt particularly unsettling.

Rod, a man in his late sixties, knew how to fix things. He was Mr Practical. He had rescued me from a bat that was flying about the living room earlier in the summer when I was home alone for a few days. Frightened, I called Rod, and he came over straight away, like someone from *Ghostbusters*, and got rid of the bat by switching off the lights and picking it up with a towel and escorting it out.

'I suggest we go over the fence and into Dai's field and pick the thing up. It may only be injured.' Simon grabbed his gardening gloves. Like Hara, Rod was someone who made me feel safe. Every problem had a solution; he dealt with life unemotionally and practically.

'Kiran – do you have a towel handy?' Rod said.

This was the start of a big operation. It was obvious that Simon, Rod and I all felt a little excited at the idea that we might be about to rescue a bird of prey. The preparation may have been minimal – gardening gloves and an old towel – but I felt it was one of those moments that reminded me that I was now living in the country. It is in such moments of contrast that we truly notice things. If they didn't exist, I fear my life would be a long stream of semi-consciousness where nothing is highlighted.

Rod and Simon, rather awkwardly, went over the wire fence and into Dai's field that sprawled out behind both our gardens. Glen had joined the party, and we both stood on the balcony of The Long Barn and viewed the rescue from above. The hawk wasn't far away – just a few feet into the field. 'It's alive!' Simon shouted out. Glen and I gave a real sigh of relief. I found it both wonderful and curious that I could feel so much relief from knowing that the bird was not dead, when ten minutes before I hadn't even known it was alive. Perhaps this was what being closer to nature was all about; that the life of those we share our planet with was felt so profoundly.

Wide open, the eyes of the hawk darted about following Simon's movements. Rod and Simon stood over the hawk and stared down at the bird that tumbled down from the sky. And in that moment, witnessed from above on the balcony, was an image that stirred me: a magnificent bird of prey fallen from the sky; man towering over bird; bird fallen from sky to Earth. Wearing gardening gloves, Simon gingerly picked up the bird; he had grown up in the countryside, outside Burton upon Trent, so he was far more comfortable in nature than me. The three of us, Rod, Glen and I, watched on apprehensively. And then there was silence. As Simon picked up the bird, its head fell to the side, its beak open and its tongue clearly visible. It was dying. Simon supported its lopsided head as Rod wrapped the towel around it. In the towel I imagined it would feel safe. It had lain on its back for at least an hour, staring at the place it fell from. Sometimes feeling safe meant minimising space, restricting movement and being still.

The bird was brought up to the balcony; we all tried not to make a fuss, but we did. How could we not; a hawk was amongst us. The sun shone brightly that afternoon as we all wondered and guessed what to do. With Simon still holding the bird and supporting its head, Glen gently pulled away a bit of the towel to inspect any injuries: it had none. On its front, breast and wings, it had down feathers – a sign of it being a young bird or a fledging; a bird that had only recently flown the nest. It was such a large bird, I found it hard to believe that it was only young. I had never seen a bird of prey so close; it looked powerful, even though it was weak. And looking at it, we understood it to be a red kite. There had been red kites nesting in the oak tree nearby.

'Hello' – it was Sarah. We often left our front door wide open in the summer. Hearing our voices, she made her way onto the balcony. And now it was the five of us wondering what to do with a red kite that looked like it was minutes away from death. Rod explained to Sarah how he came to see the bird.

'It could've had an aerial battle with a buzzard, crow or raven,' she said. We all nodded in agreement and stared at the bird.

'Its defence mechanism is to lay down and look dead,' Rod said.

A quick Google search told me that often casualties of red kites also happened when they swooped down to feast on road kill and then, being slow to fly away, got hit by cars.

Simon had handed Rod the red kite, which was still in the towel. I looked at Rod sitting down with the bird at the garden table. I felt honoured that such a magnificent creature was sitting at the table that most mornings I had my coffee at. I looked at its big claws and rather menacing yellow beak. Red kites eat carrion – dead or decaying flesh. And here it was looking half-dead but still alive.

Simon had rung up Bwlch Nant yr Arian, near Aberystwyth, which looked after red kites. He had found out about them after he messaged the community Facebook page explaining the situation. On the phone, the man at the sanctuary said it was likely that the bird had had an aerial battle, like Sarah had said. And just as Rod said, it had played dead. But the red kite had pretended to be dead for so long in the heat of the day, it had dehydrated. It was now so dehydrated that it didn't have the strength to fly away. The advice: make sure the bird is given water straight away and, if it responds well, feed it fresh meat.

As soon as Simon got off the phone, Rod, Glen, Sarah and I looked at him, as if to say what next? 'Have we got a pipette?'

Sarah ran to her house and found a pipette that she remembered was sat in her kitchen drawer. Simon went back to holding the bird, the towel wrapped around its lower half, and Rod gave it water through the pipette.

'Push it right back, Rod, to the gizzard – you need to miss the hole in its tongue; that's where it breathes from,' said Simon, now armed with information from the sanctuary.

All of us were transfixed by the bird, which was clearly gasping for water. Right before our eyes, we could see that it was coming back to life. No one said anything, but we all smiled at the bird and at each other. I couldn't believe how quick the transformation was. In a matter of minutes after drinking water, the bird no longer looked like it was on the brink of death. 'We need to give it water every 20 minutes,' Simon explained. Glen took the pipette from Rod and carried on giving it water.

It was obvious that the red kite was feeling better; it started to wriggle and it was now able to support its own head. 'Shall we give it food now?' I said. 'There's chicken in the fridge – cut it up,' Simon suggested. As I walked over to the chicken, I stopped and turned to Simon: 'But it's raw.' Everyone laughed. It was a stupid comment and, unfortunately for me, I had said it out loud. 'Kiran! I don't think it minds, darling!' Simon scoffed.

Why I was so concerned to give the red kite, which feasted on dead and decaying flesh, raw meat, I'm not quite sure. It betrayed my city roots and the disconnection I had with wildlife when it was up close. As I chopped up the raw chicken breast, I had another concern, which I kept quiet. I couldn't help but think giving it chicken was a bit like cannibalism. And when I had prepared it into tiny pieces and went out onto the balcony, I whispered in Simon's ear: 'Is it OK it's eating chicken; it doesn't feel right?' Simon whispered: 'It's OK, darling.'

With a toothpick, Sarah pierced a tiny piece of chicken flesh and fed it to the red kite. It gobbled it down in an instant. We all felt elated and carried on smiling at each other. And then she fed it some more. A few minutes later, Simon loosened the towel; the bird had started to move and wriggle. We could all see it wanted to stretch. 'I think it's about time we took the towel off the old boy,' Rod advised.

The towel was removed from the bird and draped over Simon's hand and arm to protect him from the bird's claws. The bird stood up, now fully alert. It had brightened up and started to make a high-pitched noise. I felt like clapping. What a transformation! And now it felt like it wasn't just the five of us, Simon, Rod, Glen, Sarah and me. We were now six; a bird of prey had joined the party.

The red kite stood tall and proud on Simon's arm – just like those wildlife shows where people teach you about eagles with an eagle perched on their arm. It took us all in with its beady eyes. I almost felt that we should introduce ourselves to it. I wondered what it must be thinking. There was a circle of humans and a bird, all just hanging out. We decided, now that the bird was stronger, we would escort it down to the bottom of our garden where it was wild, with long grass, nettles and brambles. So Simon walked down the iron stairs on the side of the balcony with the bird stood on his arm, as if he was escorting it to a ball. Rod followed him down. Glen, Sarah and I looked on from the balcony. The bird started to stretch its wings and flapped a little as if waking up from a deep sleep. Simon shouted that he could feel a strong and powerful pull from the bird. And before he had even reached the bottom of the garden, the red kite pulled away and flew in a slow and magical glide across the field and into the distance. We all waved and shouted 'Bye' and whispered 'Amazing'. That summer's day, when there was an abundance of life, we all held the fragility of life in our hands in the form of a bird. And then I, along with the neighbours and the bird, felt the pull of life and the need to carry on.

Something in me altered, ever so slightly, that day. Though I'm not quite sure what. Most of the things that change us are imperceptible and remain unarticulated. What I do know is that a bird of prey came and joined us on the balcony, drank water and ate a bit of chicken. It was my version of the book *The Tiger Who Came to Tea*.

AUTUMN

20

BAD NEWS

Autumn was close, I could see that the leaves of the trees had started to turn ever so slightly. Soon, the natural world would loosen its grip on everything that it had helped keep alive. It reminded me of the last autumn I had spent with my mother. In the late summer we were told that the cancer had returned. I called my mother after she had been for her regular check-up, accompanied by my sister. When I asked her what the doctors' had said, she said they told her it was back and there was nothing they could do. I felt so shocked, I couldn't understand her words; they had become complicated mathematical equations. The news had blindsided us all and we refused to believe there was no hope. So we carried on with the alternative treatments, because it was all we could do.

The truth was she was dying of cancer. We all chose not to believe it. I barely believe it now, even though she's been dead for several years. That autumn, we went out grocery shopping. Funny how life presses on with its mundanity in the face of so much. As we drove around, the autumn leaves looked particularly beautiful; they really were copper and gold. One tree was luminescent with leaves transparent and red.

'Mum, look at the trees – autumn is so beautiful!'

She soaked up the season, though she was exhausted and felt uncomfortable in the car.

'Yes, so beautiful,' was her weak reply.

I wanted her to see the beauty in life, for the last time. I wanted us to share the colours and the scent of autumn. But to admit why this was so important to me now meant that I would have to admit this would be the last of her autumns. And so I had an inner conflict about doing what was right for a dying person; to listen to the conversations that started with: 'When I'm gone . . .' But that autumn day I quietly accepted the unacceptable, and we drove around and appreciated autumn in a way neither of us ever had. We clung onto the ordinary and the everyday. It was an odd mix of appreciation of beauty in the midst of so much pain; feeling all things so wholly, so completely and so intensely. It's extraordinary how the ordinary becomes so beautiful when it's under threat. That day beauty was everywhere.

'What happens if I can't go to the bank any more?'

The afternoon was punctuated with random questions from my mother that revealed she was facing the reality of her illness. She was finding it difficult to walk now. And I answered her questions, silently admitting that we hadn't beaten cancer but that it was beating us. I stopped to buy pomegranate juice, now a regular part of her diet. Mum stayed in the car; she was feeling faint and nauseous. I went straight up to the counter to ask for what I needed; I had no time to hunt and search for it. I was so conscious of time; time could not be wasted. We only become fully aware of time when we realise we have so little of it. And then it's nearly always too late. Time is the Houdini of the metaphysical world; it escapes through the back door of our lives, although we never really felt it enter.

The shopkeeper was a man in his late sixties, and he was alone in the small shop. He told me he only had concentrated juice, but I needed fresh. I panicked. Things panicked me so easily in the days after Mum became ill. The man came away from behind the desk and tried to lead the way to the fridge.

'Let me show you dear, and then you can decide.' I didn't follow his lead. I stood rooted to my spot.

'You don't understand. My mother has cancer and she's dying, and we need fresh pomegranate juice!'

My heart broke then and there in an unfamiliar shop on a Friday afternoon, surrounded by an abundance of cereals, pot noodles, washing-up liquid, disinfectant, extra virgin olive oil and concentrated pomegranate juice. I was surrounded by domesticity. I bawled my eyes out: I had broken. The shopkeeper put his arm around me. He asked me about my family, uncles and aunts, brothers and sisters and my father. He wanted to know if my burden was shared.

'Listen young lady, life can be very hard. God bless your mother and your father. And may God give you strength.'

The man was kind and good. I left the shop without any pomegranate juice. I wiped my tears and tried to compose myself before I saw my mother. When I sat back in the car, I hoped my mother wouldn't see I had been crying. But she had wilted like a flower on the passenger seat. She was so weak. So I did what I thought was right: I drove us back and looked at the autumn trees and pointed out their beauty.

Sitting on the sofa looking at autumn approaching Wales, I wondered about the shopkeeper. I wondered if he went home that night in the autumn of 2014 and told his wife about me. Did he hug his children and wife a little bit tighter that evening? Did he allow the moments in his life to linger a little longer? Did he ever think of me like I was thinking of him now? Did he wonder about the young woman that came into his shop and insisted upon fresh pomegranate juice and then completely broke down when he said he only sold concentrated? Was he grateful for the unwanted gift that I had given him? It might have been an unwanted gift for some, my broken heart, but those who are wise would have used it well; a simple message to live wholly and completely. It might have been a story of loss and sorrow, but really it was just a love story, like any other love story. It was just that some love stories were more palatable than others, depending upon where you are in the story. But whatever the story, I believe, they all end the same.

21

BLACKBERRIES AND KITTENS

Autumn arrived like an unexpected guest. The night before, as I sat up reading in bed, in the distance I had heard an owl. I stopped reading, put down my book and listened to it. The owl sounded as though it was close by. It shared the night with a heavy, black and silent velvet sky and a gazillion stars. I felt like a child as I absorbed a moment that was sprinkled with magic. And now, looking at the unexpected guest that was autumn, I wondered if it was the owl that had called in the new season.

Staring at the valley, I realised that it had started to feel like a friend to me, a friend that would always come bearing an abundance of gifts. It gifted trees that magically transformed before my eyes; farm animals; the mellifluous whisper of the wind and all the sounds that it carried with it and a new start that came at the beginning of every new season. My heart swelled with gratitude for this gift-bearing giant that was once in moss green. Just like the circular nature of the seasons, I started to feel a curvature in my life; the soft bend of a road.

For so long, my life had felt like a straight road ahead of me; a long, hard, arduous road. I had longed for a bend. And now, looking out into what was clearly autumn, I felt the beginnings of a small and smooth curve.

Blackberries were everywhere in the autumn. Driving around, I would often see people, container in hand, collecting blackberries. The odd person would be clinging to the side of the road and inspecting the bushes for any ripe berries.

I loved how people were so appreciative of the gifts each season brought. Our local builder, Grenville, a stocky and cheerful man, lived in the local town and was a food enthusiast. He did all the renovation on The Long Barn and had become a good friend. Whenever he was at the house fixing something, inspecting something or pricing up a job, he would always make time to hang around and talk about food. He would tell us about all the things that were growing in his garden: tomatoes, potatoes, peppers, rhubarb, beetroot, onions, strawberries and garlic. He also kept chickens. His face would light up whenever he spoke about the things he was cultivating. And then he'd tell us about the things that weren't doing too well. 'Oh, my beetroot hasn't done well this year, I just don't know what the problem is.' He spoke about his vegetables with so much tenderness, it was as if he was talking about one of his children: *David hasn't done too well this year in college, I just don't know what the problem is.*

Grenville had lived in this area all his life and always had a story. Once, as we sat at the kitchen table drinking coffee, he told me a story of an old farming couple who he had worked for over the years. He said that the couple only ever cooked two meals. In the summer, they would eat the fruits of their labour – salads made from the vegetables they had grown. And in the autumn and winter, they would have cawl, considered to be the national dish of Wales. Cawl is a broth consisting of pieces of lamb and vegetables: potatoes, leeks, swede and carrots, though these can vary depending upon which part of Wales you're in. The old farming couple cooked cawl in an old cast-iron pot.

'The pot wasn't washed. What happened, you see, is that they just added to the pot everyday.'

I imagined the cast-iron pot giving a constant supply of cawl – a pot that just kept on giving.

'I know that when I make a curry, it always tastes better the next day and the day after,' I said. Grenville nodded enthusiastically.

'This would be the same for cawl. But this isn't unusual in these parts, Kiran, eating the same food almost every day. This is common amongst the old Welsh.'

I'd eaten cawl a number of times since I moved here. It was served in a big hearty bowl and accompanying it would be a small bit of cheese and a piece of crusty bread. I imagined that, in the cold, wet and harsh winters in Wales, cawl would be wholesome and filling. Grenville continued with my Welsh lesson.

'It's a peasant dish – there's no fixed recipe written down, just families handing down the recipe from family to family.'

I imagined what 'peasant food' from around the world would be similar to cawl. Perhaps Irish stew?

Grenville got up to leave. 'I hope you're making the best of the blackberries. I collected a whole lot the other day. I'll be making blackberry jam and blackberry and apple crumble.'

I'd never been blackberry picking and now I was surrounded by them. 'That's what I'll do this afternoon, Grenville, I will go blackberry picking and make an apple and blackberry crumble!' Grenville smiled. I think he enjoyed teaching me about the area and the ways I could enjoy its riches.

That afternoon, in my Little Red Riding Hood raincoat, I left the house to go blackberry picking. There was a real satisfaction in going out foraging and then making something delicious from what you had found. In a matter of a few hours, something that was growing on a bush would end up in a pie dish served with custard.

I took a small Tupperware container and walked down towards Dai's farmhouse. The blackberry bushes were on the sides of the winding road. I occasionally stopped to check on a bush to see if it had any berries worth picking. Some had obviously been eaten by the birds and some were just infested with insects. I felt a slight revulsion from looking at berries half-eaten by insects and those that were rotting. I felt embarrassed that I couldn't get over this part of me; I was too used to produce coming in well-presented and brilliantly packaged boxes. I didn't want to be that person. It was the same feeling I had had when I watched the slaughtering of the pigs –

I no longer wanted to think of them coming from aisle No. 9 in Sainsbury's. So I carried on looking for the berries, even though I was scared of the spiders and the advanced stages of decay made my skin crawl.

I passed a little stream that ran alongside the bushes on the side of the road. It was about metre in width. The berries that were there were the best I had seen that afternoon. In order to pick them, I'd have to teeter on the edge of the stream and push myself forward. I found myself in a diagonal position: my hands against the bush, still holding my Tupperware container, and my feet on tiptoe on the edge of the stream. I had overstretched.

A car passed by and I half-smiled, embarrassed by the awkward position I found myself in. I was glad it wasn't anyone I knew. I then fell into the stream. My feet submerged in cold water. I wished I were wearing wellies and not my walking boots. Things that live in streams – silt, mud and bits that were once part of a tree – encased my feet and water entered my shoes. 'Bloody hell!' I yelled. But I wasn't hurt and was grateful that I hadn't twisted my ankle. There was a time I would have walked back home in a defeated grump, but I jumped out back onto the road and picked up my fallen container, feeling even more determined to find those damn berries.

With sodden feet, I carried on walking down the road in search of autumn's gifts. And as I passed Dai's open barn on my right I noticed two little black dots. I stopped and stared. In front of me were two tiny black kittens. I couldn't see them properly, but they were there. I tried to get closer and slowly made my way towards them, but they scurried away upon my approach. They jumped, bounced and leapt; two black dots like two energetic full stops.

The kittens were tiny. And for a few minutes, the kittens and I stared at each other in silent chatter: *Who are you? What's your name?* I knew from a conversation that I had had with one of the locals that kittens born in the autumn are known as 'blackberry kittens'. I could have stared at them all day, but the kittens disappeared into barn. I was so transfixed, I wanted to follow them. But the bark of a dog coming from Dai's farmhouse close to the barn told me not to. I turned back and walked home with an empty Tupperware container but with a heart full of kittens.

That evening, I visited Dai's farmhouse. In the house was Dai's wife Miar and Dai's brother. I asked Miar about the kittens – she knew straight away which ones they were and told me they were about five weeks old. I was happy to wait for a few weeks for the kitten to get bigger, but Miar said the mother was neglectful of the kittens and Miar was bottle-feeding them.

The next day, I went over to Dai's farmhouse to drop off a pet carrier for when the kitten was ready. I was so excited at the idea of having an eight-week-old kitten. When I arrived, Miar told me she had already got the kitten for me and it was in the shed in a transportable cat basket. We all went to the shed, and when I looked into the basket, there were two kittens.

'What happened was, when we put the kitten in the shed ready for you, the other kitten stood crying outside the shed.

She wouldn't leave her sister. She was missing her.' There was no option but to take them both and I was secretly pleased.

We got the kittens home and put them in our kitchen in a large cage just until they got settled. We also wanted to introduce the kittens slowly to Truffle, our old cat from London. Although the kittens were identical, their personalities were very different – one was feisty and the other a little reserved and timid. We named them Waterloo and Paddington, a nod to London stations. The first day we had them was so exciting – a rambunctious couple of farm kittens. I would give them a good home; plenty of food, love and attention. I almost felt that they had been presented to me; they needed me and I needed them.

We had them less than 24 hours when we noticed something was wrong with the kitten that was reserved, Paddington. She seemed to be in a lot of pain; she was crying and throwing herself around in the cage. When we tried to pick her up, she recoiled. It was Sunday morning and we called the vet, and were asked to bring her in for an emergency appointment. She cried all the way to the vets and I couldn't help but think that the movement of the car was making her pain worse. The vet said Paddington had a birth defect – her intestines and gut were twisted, which is why she was in pain. We now understood why she had been reserved and much quieter than her sister. They could operate on her, but she was so young and delicate, she probably wouldn't make it through the op. We were told that the kindest thing we could do was to put her down. So we did.

I sobbed when the vet told us that we should put Paddington

to sleep, so I sat in the car with Waterloo and Simon stayed with Paddington and the vet. I thought about that morning and how Paddington was throwing herself about. I had watched her take herself to the litter tray, in the corner of the cage; even when she was suffering, she still wanted to do the right thing. For some reason, I found this heartbreaking: she was a determined little creature. The plan had been to give the kitten a happy new life full of love and attention – not for us to put her down as soon as she arrived! It cost us nothing to take her from the farm, but £100 to end her life. The vet said that if she had stayed on the farm, she would have had a long, drawn-out, painful death. And she most probably would have been taken by a buzzard or a fox in her eventual slowed-down state.

I was shocked at how much I cried in the car for a kitten I had only known since yesterday. I expected to feel sad, but not this uncontrollable state of sobbing. Where there was once two there was now one. I thought about what Miar had told me: when she had put one of the kittens in the cage in the shed, the other one stood outside, crying for her sister. I had taken both so that they wouldn't have to part, and now they were separated forever. A lifeline cut.

I thought about the red kite and how it swiftly flew across the field and disappeared into the sky it had fallen from. I thought about the slaughtering of the pigs and how I thanked the pig as it lay on my plate as sweet and sour pork. I thought about the owl I had heard the other night and how it made me feel some kind of magic. And then my mind came back to poor Paddington.

I felt a transformation in me. I had always felt some separation between myself and the world; I had always been an observer of it, a voyeur of sorts, though I had always lived sensitively within it. But the mesh between the world and myself had been lifted, and life permeated my existence in a way it had never done before.

The vet had given us the option of taking Paddington home or they would dispose of her tiny body themselves. She may have only been in our lives a day and a bit, but she had a home and it was ours, so we took her back. I apologised to Waterloo: *I'm sorry we couldn't save your sister.* And I apologised to Paddington just before Simon buried her in our garden where vegetables and flowers flourished.

We had to change the name Waterloo; there couldn't be a Waterloo without a Paddington. So she was now Blackberry.

22

THE BEGINNINGS OF THINGS
AND THE ENDS OF THINGS

Autumn always reminded me of going back to school, no matter how far away my schooldays were. There is one prominent memory. It's 1986 and I am 11 years old. There are conkers everywhere. I have collected many, washed them and now they're all shiny and new. At school, the teachers have asked us all to bring fruit and vegetables to take to the local church to celebrate harvest. The local church happens to be the church my mother and father got married in. We draw pictures of fruit to hang up in church. I draw a picture of a mango; it has all the colours of a sunset. Some children bring tins of fruit too. My mother gives me apples to take to school. She watches me through the window as I leave the front door. I turn around and she waves at me.

Standing in the garden, I crawled out of my memory of harvest time at school, even though it was warm with all the colours of autumn: gold, red, purple and orange. Like a cloud heavy with rain, I felt a pull on my heart. I was aware when my mother died that my future would change and would be different from the one I imagined. But there is something that I was unprepared for. No one tells you that your past goes through its own metamorphosis. We are told that you can't change the past, but when a loved one dies, not only does your future change, your past changes too. You view it from the vantage point of an experience that cracked you open like a nut. Simple memories become painful because they exist in the past with the knowledge that there is no future. Nothing can change the past – until death becomes a bookend to your memories.

The beginning of autumn was a funny time. The trees started to lose their leaves, but our baskets were full of fruit and vegetables. It was a season of both giving and taking; like life, a balance of both holding on and letting things go. That morning, Jane had dropped off a few jars of marmalade she had made. 'I will be pickling beetroot next week – I'll drop some by.' This idea of preserving things for the winter when there would no longer be an abundance of produce was new to me. This was the first time I had really lived within the constraints of the seasons; where a season's character was acknowledged and accepted. In the city I had been fed from a conveyor belt of food, whether it was in season or not. But this way of living somehow made the fruit we picked taste sweeter.

Basket in hand, I picked things for the evening dinner: onions, garlic and carrots; I was making cawl. I inspected the onions and wondered whether those whose younger years had been tainted with sadness lived forever in their childhoods, longing for something that always seemed so perfect in others? Other children's lives always seemed so carefree, as you would expect a child's to be. My childhood was so adult, as it is for children of alcoholics. You never know what you are coming home to: an ogre you have to flee from or a parent who is sober. Other children's lives always appeared so idyllic compared to mine, as if they belonged in storybooks. So I preferred to read stories of faraway lands, which meant there was no room for comparison. I took to writing stories in an attempt to make sense of the world; scribbling sentences in a journal – the beginnings of something and the ends of something, like a squirrel hoarding nuts.

A friend asked how I could forgive my father and continue my relationship with him when he spent so much of my childhood letting me down. As an adult, the question was easy to answer. In childhood, parents are our first experience of God; they give us life, look over us and protect us from the harsh realities of living in the world. As long as we see them as such, there is no room for forgiveness: gods do not fail. When I became an adult, I saw my father first and foremost as a human being, and as soon as I saw him as just that, it was easy to forgive. He was a mere man, a person just as messed up as the rest of us. As a kid, I read a book on Greek mythology. I realised my father was not a god, as I had known a god to be, but a Greek god, capable of error and destruction. When I was a little girl, I realised that adults were fallible and that I was the creator of my own little world. Instead of being frightened by the enormity of the revelation, I found it freeing and swallowed the idea whole, like an oyster, as I intended to do with all the other worlds I encountered.

Our onions were good, and I placed four in the basket. We had both red and white; red onions for curries and white for everything else. Our small pear and apple trees didn't have much fruit. A few days ago I had walked up the road to post a letter and when I arrived back home I discovered six sheep in our front garden. They were eating our spinach and the apples and pears on the lower branches. They had come from the back of the house and Dai's field after discovering a hole in the wire fence. At first I just stood on top of the drive and stared at the sheep helping themselves to our fruit and vegetables. They didn't seem to notice I was there. I ran down the drive waving my hands in the air and shouting like a mad woman. The sheep remained unperturbed. I then jumped up and down, arms and legs moving in some kind of tribal dance. The sheep rushed past me, nearly knocking me over, and disappeared up the drive. The garden was a mess with sheep droppings. But in a way, I was quite happy that the sheep had visited. They were visitors, just as the brown rabbit, the dragonflies, frogs, magpies and red kites were. It didn't sit well with me to feel ownership over the outside space. It belonged to us all.

I moved to the second raised vegetable bed where the carrots and peas grew. It was a satisfying job pulling vegetables up from the ground, unearthing them and exposing them to the full light of day. I noticed that the carrot I pulled was split into two;

it divided at the bottom into two separate roots. Grenville told me this happened because the carrot would have met an obstacle, a rock or something, so it worked its way around it to continue its growth. Between finger and thumb, I dangled the carrot in front of me. Staring at it, it was the perfect example of the expression 'where there's a will, there's a way'. It found its way around the obstacles; its road diverged into two. I thought about all the things that flourished in life in spite of other things that tried to stop them. Life was a force that was simply pushing through.

The garlic grew in the same bed as the spring onions and spinach. I knelt down and put my basket to the side. Sat in the bed, the garlic looked like round Chinese dumplings. They were propped up as if they had unearthed themselves, ready for the world. I grabbed a few bulbs; they fitted perfectly in the palm of my hand. One really notices when something fits. I threw the bulbs in my basket and a whiff of earth tickled my nose. It smelt like Home; perhaps not home, but just something that was so familiar to me. Earth to earth, ashes to ashes, dust to dust. For some reason, my hands wanted to keep searching the soil, even though I had picked all that I needed. So I put both hands into the ground, like a child playing in a sand pit, and the aroma of the earth, laced with the faint smell of autumn, made its way into my nostrils and made me feel whole. I enjoyed the smell of being so close to the earth. I realised that sometimes participating in life meant standing still in it.

I dug deeper. My hands pushed through soil and passed

earthworms. I imagined that if I dug deep enough, I'd break into the crust of the Earth; the mantle and then the outer and finally the inner core. And perhaps like this I would break in and discover the code of life itself. It wasn't good enough for me to just think and feel my way through the days and the years. Since I was a child, I had an innate desire to know all things. I think this came from belonging to a family where many ran on faith alone. I rebelled; I wanted to know why the world was round and not just believe it to be. I wanted to see the deep depths of the ocean, the pyramids and the man on the moon. I wanted to taste life. And I wanted life to taste me. My grandfather, the pastor, would preach about the dangers of the world; to him it was full of landmines. The way he felt about the world was just how Wilf felt about London: best avoided. But for me, the world roused feelings of wonder and mysticism. It held me in the palm of its hand, and I was dazzled by it.

23

ANDREW AND THE SAS

The Special Air Service (SAS) trains in the Brecon Beacons, a mountain range in South Wales. It would be easy to forget that the SAS and the army were present if it hadn't been for the odd fighter jet that occasionally tore up the sky. The incongruous sound that cut into the country air had at first alarmed me, but like most things, I got used to it, and it joined the rest of the sounds that existed in my new life.

It has been reported that as many as 20 soldiers have died during the SAS selection process in the Brecon Beacons, many due to heatstroke from their gruelling training. According to figures, almost one soldier has died every two years in the mountain range since 1984.

The range has six main peaks, and is said to be named after the ancient practice of lighting signal fires (beacons) on the tops of mountains to ward off attacks from invaders. The presence of the SAS in the Welsh mountains gave the beauty of the mountain range a savage quality. The landscape reminded me of a trek I had done in Crete years prior, when I had visited the gorge of Samaria. We had trekked for several hours before we reached the beautiful gorge, which immediately held me to ransom: I had become its prisoner. Mountains have a habit of holding people captive . . .

Andrew, from across the valley, told me a story that he had become an unwilling participant to. One late autumn, he had been home alone. He watched TV and a film, while eating a dinner of chicken and mushroom pie, peas and chips. After finishing his dinner, he watched a film and then ate the leftovers from his meal for one.

He said he had felt a little chilly; the autumn sun had warmed the house during the day, but now, at 9pm, he felt the season's cold embrace. He couldn't sleep and decided to watch another film, but first he would light the fire. He walked out of his front door to collect some wood that he had been chopping all year round ready for the cold months. He enjoyed using his chainsaw; he said a day without his chainsaw was a day wasted.

He stepped out into the glare of a full moon. The outbuildings, two rather large sheds and a substantial polytunnel, all shone bright, illuminated by the moon. It was a hushed, quiet night where all things stood still in their rightful places. Cocooned by the serenity of the evening, Andrew leisurely walked over to the shed that housed all the seasoned wood. He opened the door and immediately heard a rattling noise. He thought nothing of it – rats, feral cats?

As he walked in, he noticed that there were two grown men

sat in the corner of the shed. Andrew said he hadn't jumped, he didn't make a sound. But there had been a quiet exchange, an acknowledgement between all three of them. And in what he said could have been minutes but in reality was seconds, they all drank in each other's presence. He said he wasn't sure why he hadn't jumped in surprise – I said I would have screamed. Perhaps knowing that everything was being watched by a full moon comforted him.

In the silence of their exchange, the two men got up rather clumsily and made their way towards the door. In a polite dance of exchanges, Andrew moved away from the door as the two men approached stealthily. And without words or gestures, they walked out of the shed and Andrew followed, mesmerised by his findings. In the light of the full moon, Andrew could clearly see that the men were wearing identical dark clothing: big long coats and huge boots. And even though he stood 12 feet away from them, he could smell them. One of the men nodded at the house, indicating that they would like to go in. Andrew didn't think twice about it, ran ahead and opened the front door of his house. And then they were all inside.

'Got any food?' one of them said. 'Oh yes, peas, chips and a pie.' As soon as Andrew said those words, he realised that were no chips, peas or pie. He had eaten all the leftovers. He apologised. Andrew said he wasn't quite sure why he had been so apologetic to the two strangers who had crept their way out of his shed just moments before. Despite their well-built bodies, he could tell they were famished and he could detect a sense of desperation about them. That day, Andrew had bought potatoes and the bag sat unopened on the kitchen worktop. One of the men grabbed the potatoes and ripped open the bag. He took hold of two potatoes and bit into them as though they were apples. The second man followed and they bit chunks off the raw potatoes as if they hadn't eaten for weeks.

Andrew just stood and stared in disbelief. Breaking his silence, he said, 'Fancy a fry-up?' The two men nodded enthusiastically while they chomped away on their raw potatoes.

Andrew found some bacon in the fridge and the eggs he had got the day before from his neighbour's chickens. He hurriedly made the strangers dinner. If he didn't hurry, he'd be forcing them to eat more of the potatoes, and he didn't want to be responsible for that. As he cracked open the eggs, the two men told Andrew they were from the SAS and were on their training. They avoided answering any questions from Andrew of where they had come from and how long they had been on their special mission. He soon realised he shouldn't ask any more questions; they only told him what they wanted him to know. Their words were measured, as if they were only allowed to utter a set number of words.

They finished off a whole packet of bacon, the box of six eggs and the last pieces of sliced bread.

At midnight one of the men said: 'We'll sleep here, downstairs.'

Andrew nodded and obediently went upstairs to his room. He was happy to be out of sight, but there was a danger in not being able to witness what they might be up to. He sat up in bed and thought about the two SAS men downstairs: if they wanted, they could kill him. Thoughts of the ways you could kill someone in their sleep occupied Andrew's mind for most of the night. If he were murdered right now, no one would know. His screams would be swallowed by the inky-blue, moon-filled sky. In his panic, he wondered whether the moon acted like a lid that muffled noise. The moon was responsible for a lot of things, such as ocean tides – what else could it be responsible for? He had never imagined his days would end like this: a small part in an escapade involving two SAS men. They had been friendly enough and they enjoyed the fry-up that he had made, but still, he didn't know them – they were strangers and potential killing machines. What was he doing? More importantly, what were they doing? That night, the sound of the two men snoring comforted Andrew. If they were snoring, they were sleeping and he was safe.

'I think I only just fell asleep when they entered my room at 5am,' Andrew told me.

They asked him to get up and drive them to a spot 30 miles away. Andrew was obedient; he was happy that they were leaving. The car wouldn't start that morning and Andrew cursed the car that had been so reliable all the other times. Once the car had started, the two men sat in the back seats. 'Just drive until we tell you not to.'

And so Andrew followed the instructions from the two SAS men. He didn't feel comfortable that he was driving out into the hills. He had grown up looking at these very hills, but now they didn't look so friendly.

'Slow down, keep it at 30. Andrew slowed down to 30mph.

And then the strangest thing happened: both men opened the back-seat passenger doors and rolled out of the car. Andrew carried on driving away from the spot that he had dropped them at, just like they said he should.

A month later, Andrew received an anonymous card in the post with a simple message: *Thanks.* Inside the card was £40.

24

WILF AND HIS FAVOURITE MEAL

I was finding autumn a lovely time to go walking. The sun sat in the right place, and it didn't feel oppressive as it did in the summer. Sitting in his little white van one afternoon, I saw Wilf eating his packed lunch. I was going on one of my long walks; I was feeling restless and needed to stretch my legs. I had also baked a lemon drizzle cake and wrapped a slice in foil to give to Wilf, so I was pleased when I saw him. The window of the van was open; it would be very unlike Wilf to shut out the outside. With the backdrop of a perfect autumn country scene, his white van looked almost beautiful; a John Constable painting with a splash of modernity.

'Hello, Wilf!' I shouted before I had even reached his van.

I was excited to see him, excited to give him cake, and took giant steps approaching him. Sometimes the countryside made me feel lonely. My mind would take me across valleys, streams and forests, and the wild barrenness of it all, depending upon my mood, would overwhelm me. And I would be left with a strong feeling of needing to connect. I gave him the cake and he placed it on the passenger side. He said 'Excellent' and then 'Thank you'.

Wilf was drinking out of one of those big wide enamel mugs that campers used. I could see he was having soup for lunch. Bedside him, on the passenger seat, was a homemade sandwich made with white bread. I wondered what was inside the sandwich.

'Oooh, soup for lunch?!'

'Yes, and fish paste sandwiches.'

This made me smile. His lunch sounded so old-fashioned, comforting and homely. Something my deceased grandfather would have had. Being a foodie, I asked him what he was having for his dinner.

'Oh, I know exactly what I'm having. I've been eating the same dinner for ten years.'

'For ten years? The same dinner? For ten years?' I asked in disbelief. I was horrified and intrigued at the same time. To me, life was a banquet, and I always showed up for the feasting.

'Yes . . . yes . . . I have a routine, just like nature, you see. I've had the same supper for ten years.'

'Even on Christmas Day? Surely not.'

'Even on Christmas Day. It's like any other day for a farmer. The sheep have to get fed – they don't ask for anything different.'

But you're not a sheep, Wilf, I thought.

I imagined Wilf on Christmas Day. He looked the same: blue overalls and conspicuously missing a Christmas cracker paper hat. I knew I always had trouble imagining Wilf in a domestic setting, away from his shed, sheep and fields, and now with this new information I could see why. He was like a stick of rock; the uniformity of his life ran all the way through him. I had so many questions and tried not to blurt them out all at once. I didn't want to run the risk of making Wilf feel awkward by revealing my shock and surprise at this latest information. It was never my intention to ever make him feel awkward. I was intrigued by him; he was unlike anyone I had ever met, and I had so much to learn. It was me who lived awkwardly; I wore life like an ill-fitting Christmas jumper.

'Well, what is it?'

'What is what?'

'The meal you've been having for ten years?'

What could possibly taste that good for someone to commit to eating it for a decade? I was desperate to know what this spellbinding meal that stopped Wilf exploring all other foods consisted of. The sweet taste of lobster? Scallops with bacon lardons accompanied by a pea purée? Beef Wellington with dauphinoise potatoes?

'I have two pieces of fish, one onion, an egg, baked beans and a few biscuits at the end. For lunch, I have a pear, an orange and four sandwiches with paste. But sometimes, when it gets cold, I'll have a cup of soup too.'

I laughed and smiled at his choice of meal and at the occasional simplicity of life. This was Wilf's winning dinner. He wasn't just wedded to the land, he was also married to this one supper. Wilf had lodged himself into his life so that it ran like clockwork. He wasn't consumed by the everyday decisions most people had to make. He was free of the smaller details of our lives; he never asked what's for lunch or dinner. The meal itself sounded fine – there was nothing outlandish about it; I could eat it myself. This was all such a revelation to me. I always thought variety was the spice of life, and here was Wilf happily telling me about the sameness of his.

I imagined Wilf biting into an onion like someone would bite into an apple. As if he read my mind, Wilf said: 'The onions are my favourite part most of all. I slice the onion and fry it.'

He smiled as he talked about his decade-long meal. This was something I could relate to – food made me happy too.

Wilf gulped a bit of soup and carried on talking. Unusually, he was in a rather chatty mood and, as always, I was happy to listen to him. I always felt the wonderful warm glow of a child at story time when he spoke. I was an attentive listener.

'When I go to the supermarket, I know exactly what I want. I'm not interested in other food.'

'Have you ever had Indian food?'

'I've never had Chinese, Indian or French food. Why change? I've already found the food I love. It would be a job to alter me. I think I had pizza once – Italian isn't it?'

Wilf reasoned that because he had found the food he loved, there was no need to try anything else. Although this wasn't something I could ever imagine doing myself, I both admired and was envious of this simple logic. What if we all found what we were looking for, as Wilf had? What would happen next? Would we all stop seeking and stop still in the satisfaction that we had now found what made us happy?

The philosopher Arthur Schopenhauer said 'possession takes away the charm'. He believed that as soon as we possessed what we desired, we would get bored and move onto our next want; we would never stop wanting. I always thought this to be true of human nature, that in life the proverbial carrot is forever dangled. But this wasn't true of Wilf. He broke all the rules that I thought were part of being human; he was free of them – an unlikely anarchist dismantling the laws of nature.

Standing by Wilf's van and talking to him through his open window as he ate his lunch seemed innocuous enough. But the conversation had solidified our differences once more; we were both worlds of contrasts, never quite merging. And like the autumn leaves that had just started to fall, our words danced between us: hypnotic and curious.

'My uncle, a bachelor and a farmer like me, had the same food for every meal! He had bread, butter, cheese and tea for breakfast, lunch and dinner. When I would visit him, he would bring out the jam. The jam would always come out for the visitors!' Wilf added.

I laughed and I was relieved to see that we were both laughing; even Wilf could see the eccentricity of it all. He continued to talk about his eating habits and how every Friday he would take the bus to Aberystwyth to go to the supermarket, Lidl. 'There's no responsibility on the bus, you see,' he said. He enjoyed the freedom the bus ride gave him. The variety of goods and people in the supermarket made him think of the idiosyncratic nature of the world. 'Going to Lidl just makes me think about how many people must be in this world! Crikey, so many people!' he said.

This small supermarket, in a town that was definitely not cosmopolitan, was Wilf's gateway to foreign lands and adventure. Every Friday, via an old slow country bus, he was catapulted into the centre of the world. It was his chance to walk amongst a marketplace of new food, people and ideas. He was finally part of the cacophony; looking from the inside out. It was his small window into a world that didn't belong to him but was happy to visit every Friday. I tried to imagine Wilf in London or the streets of New York. He'd be out of place; a misfit amongst misfits, swearing and loud Londoners or New Yorkers who forgot to smile. Often, the true beauty of things shone brightest when they were misplaced, like the moon during the day. I had a strong desire to take Wilf by the hand and show him a different world; my world through my eyes, just as he was showing me his. Would he hate it or love it? Would he eventually blend into it or remain on the periphery, floating like oil over water? Would he see me differently having seen the places I had occupied, knowing that these places, foreign and harsh, lived inside me?

I bid Wilf farewell and let him get on with his lunch of paste sandwiches and soup.

Just as I turned to continue with my walk, Wilf shouted.

'Look around you, those line of trees!' He was pointing towards the forest.

'Yes?'

'In 12 days, they will be filled with the colours of autumn.'

I believed him. Back in spring he had told me that I would hear the cuckoo in ten days, and he was right, I did.

I walked up to the Roman road and wrestled with what I had just learnt about Wilf. I was challenged by his very existence; it went against all I knew about living a good life. A good life, I thought, was one that was well travelled and full of experience of other foods and cultures. He was rooted; stuck in his ways; never tried news things; hardly stepped out of the small circumference of his life. He was limited. He was happy.

I reached the Roman road, then turned left and looked down the long road ahead of me. The autumn afternoon sun hung low in the sky making it feel friendlier from when it hung high in the months of summer. In the summer, the sun glared down at me from its elevated position; hanging low, as it did now, the sun walked along beside me. I tried to enjoy the autumn and see it through Wilf's eyes, but since my mother died, I was afraid of it. It was filled with a sense of foreboding; Christmas was around the corner, followed by memories of my winter of discontent. A winter that I accepted would stay my whole life. In December 2014, when my mum died, I had entered the world of Narnia: always winter, but never Christmas.

I walked slowly down the road. I didn't want to rush my walk; all around me nature was shutting down. There was a faint sweet smell, almost imperceptible, of leaves and vegetation starting to rot. Years ago, I wouldn't have noticed it. The ash and beech trees had already started to turn. The cuckoo had long gone back to Africa, but birds such as teal, snipe and lapwing would soon be arriving on the Teifi marshes. The swifts, swallows and house martins that had provided the soundtrack to our summer would be preparing for winter by migrating to Africa. We had seen their fledglings being taught how to catch flies on the wing. We had watched them grow and learn. Things were coming and going. The vigour of summer was truly over.

I reached the less barren part of my walk and passed a couple of odd houses with wild gardens. A swarm of wasps crowded a few wild plum trees that had dropped their fruit. The wasps were particularly aggressive this time of year, intoxicated by fermented fruit. I picked up my stride, hoping to avoid their drunken rampage.

Thinking about Wilf's eternal and restrictive dinner made me think of my own eating habits. Most of the time, I tried not to eat the things that made me happy, so in a way, I curbed my own happiness. I tried not to eat cheese, crisps, cakes, desserts and chocolate, although I failed miserably at doing so. Then, like the rising sun, it dawned on me: it was me who was restricted in my eating habits, not Wilf. Wilf was eating the food he loved every night, unapologetically. He wasn't restricting himself; quite the contrary. Every night he celebrated being alive by rewarding himself his favourite meal. His chosen plat du jour: happiness.

Two pieces of fish, one onion, an egg and baked beans, Wilf had said. I thought about all the things that had happened in the decade of Wilf eating his favourite meal: the death of my mother, my father losing his mind, the severed ties with my siblings and other members of family and leaving London. These had been transformative years for me, and all the while, Wilf had been creating his favourite meal for supper every night of those years. There was comfort to be had in the ordinariness and the uniformity of life.

Years ago, I had seen an article in one of the Sunday papers called 'The Last Supper', featuring a series of photographs of the last meals people ate just before they were executed. The article stayed in my head long after I had read it. It made me think about how ritualistic and ceremonial the ordinary task of having supper was. The setting-up of the table; placing down the cutlery; the positioning of cutlery to indicate you had finished your meal; the little things we did without question. I couldn't work out if there was a peculiar savagery in asking someone who was about to be executed what they would like for their last supper; inviting them to take their last bite of life. But I was certain, whatever they chose, it would taste bitter. I thought about what I would choose: it varied between a Sunday roast or a lamb curry with rice. Away from death row, most people wouldn't be aware that it was their last supper they were eating, so would have no choice in it. But it was guaranteed that Wilf would have his favourite last supper.

25

WRITER'S BLOCK

In the late autumn, I fell into a well of silence. I'm not quite sure when I had tripped and fallen, but I was swimming in circles. It was as if my very being had decided to hibernate along with the bats, hedgehogs and dormice. I had a severe case of writer's block. I was a journalist. Words were my livelihood.

My writer's block came in the form of a full stop. I awoke one morning and found it standing beside me. It followed me to the bathroom and then to every other room that I sat in. It never left my sight. In my study, while I sat at my desk, the full stop stretched out on the chaise longue. I looked out of the window and counted sheep. I could do anything, except write. Work deadlines swiftly passed me by and words escaped me. My country walks, which often sparked inspiration or at least clarity of thought, just left me feeling empty. The landscape and my heart no longer spoke to each other; the countryside looked desolate to me now, and I was poorer for it. I couldn't see the colours of the autumn; all I could see were the leaves that had fallen. It did little to dislodge the blockage in my brain. I lived in a wordless bubble; a sac of amniotic fluid where everyday life no longer penetrated my existence. I had been here before; a barrier of protection between me and the outside. But before, the exile had been my decision. This time, I had slipped and fallen into what felt like the open mouth of a grave.

Weeks went by, and my body became hunched and gnarly. I looked morose; knitted eyebrows and a pensive stare. The full stop in my life had become a huge wall that I couldn't abseil. It followed me everywhere, this huge ugly breeze-block wall. I had once read how philosopher Jean-Paul Sartre, as part of his research on a writing one of his books, had experimented with mescaline. For weeks he was plagued with seeing imaginary crabs. The crabs followed him everywhere, in the streets and when he taught in class. He got so used to them, he'd greet them every morning with: 'Good morning, my little ones, how did you sleep?' I had lived with the full stop for weeks, and I couldn't imagine befriending it, as Sartre had his crabs, and accepting it as if it were an extension of myself. Since it had arrived, it had bottled me, muted me, assuring that nothing flowed in or out. Having tried everything from socialising to solitary walks, I locked myself away in The Long Barn in a self-imposed exile in a self-built cocoon waiting for something to dislodge.

Sarah would occasionally pop her head in after work to enquire, 'Have you still got your writer's block?'

'Yes.'

'Poor thing! Now, don't go back into your study – just leave it for a few days.' A few days had turned into a few weeks.

When Simon opened the front door for the postman, Nigel, to deliver a parcel, Nigel asked: 'Are things still bad?' And Simon confirmed that they were: 'Not a word has been written.' In the supermarket I had bumped into Glen: 'I hope things get better for you soon.'

My writer's block became the topic of conversation; it was as if there had been a little death. Sentences like, 'Aw, must be terrible for her' or 'Let her know we're thinking of her' and 'I can't imagine what that must feel like' were thrown around; mournful laments uttered so freely.

In a way, it was a death; a death of a person that I identified as and how others saw me: a writer. What was a writer who could no longer write? When my family imploded, I struggled with the concept of identity. Now, I was beginning to find out that it's possible to get stuck in an identity and turn it into something that imprisons you. How you identify yourself becomes so rigid that its absence throws you. No longer free-flowing, we become rigid – defined by external things. And all these things that are outside ourselves, that we rely so heavily on to make us who we are, become our human scaffolding, holding us up, giving us the shape that we present to the world. But what happens when our defining element disappears, when what once defined us leaves us? Who was Wilf without his sheep, his supper and his lush green hills? Humans are fragile creatures; they live in glasshouses. They are defined by things that they themselves may not have acknowledged, leaving them vulnerable.

One morning, a strong wind arrived in the valley and didn't leave. It hugged the mountains and hills in an invisible embrace, and in doing so, it held us all captive. It was a wind that, much like pain, demanded to be felt. Tornadoes of leaves surrounded the house and all the nice furniture on the balcony crashed into each other and turned inside out. The lights in the barn flickered on and off, our power cables being overhead, not underground. Trees that had stood for hundreds of years uprooted and fell to the ground, blocking roads, stopping the cattle and people getting on with the daily chore of living. The trees were removed by some of the people in the valley. They got their chainsaws out and carefully sawed the tree trunks and slowly unblocked the roads. The trees were then cut up into pieces and distributed to those who wanted it so that they could keep their fires lit and their houses warm. Witnessing this camaraderie reminded me of a documentary I had seen, where a whale had been beached in a small town in Alaska. The busy town had been hushed by the presence of the whale, as though the sea had regurgitated an ancient deity. The quiet that had set in was like a fog of silence, as things do become silent when something beguiling and magnificent falls. The beached whale was then cut up and shared amongst the people in the town. Nothing was wasted. We didn't have majestic whales, but we had ancient trees that had been uprooted. Both were giants that fell.

I sat in my study with the full stop and stared out of the window and counted sheep again. I heard a knock on the front door and then the sound of it opening. I wondered what the wind had brought in.

'Hello?' I recognised the voice – it was Sophie, a woman in her late forties who lived in the valley and worked at a horse-riding school.

'I'm in here!' I shouted.

Sophie walked into the study, struggling, carrying something cumbersome. Her brown hair was a mess; the wind had blown it in various directions and her cheeks were crimson. I felt the chill in the day bounce off her and lay its hands upon me. 'I hope you don't mind, but I was thinking about your writer's block and thought I might be able to help you.' I looked at the thing she was carrying: it was a massage table. Sophie was a trained masseur.

'Oh, how lovely,' I said as I stood up to hug her.

'Well, it might help, you never know.'

In my study, we set up the massage table and played Classic FM and lit a few candles. Lying down on my stomach, my eyes were closed to the outside world, but the howl of the wind was still present and whispered in my ears. Something in the universe sounded wild and unfamiliar. The wind had stayed so long, it had become part of our lives that month of autumn, and no one mentioned how windy it was any more. It was a wild dog that had been let loose, roaming the hills and the mountains, and all we could do was wait for it to exhaust itself. It added to the mythical nature of the hills; folklore and fairy tales. 'The Lark

Ascending' started to play on the radio. My body relaxed into the melodic sound of my favourite piece of music, and I allowed myself to feel again. I was no longer up against the breeze-block full stop.

Sophie pressed into my back, which, overnight, had started to feel old. A twisted and aching body that had left all the certainties and constraints of life in search of truth and freedom. I was missing the exuberance of London. My life felt like the fields that surrounded me: a sea of endless green with no notable markings or places to stop. I missed the spontaneity of the city; the museums, the plethora of restaurants and the constant chatter. Internally I had settled into a quietude, and externally there was much of the same. There was too much silence, and not enough contrast.

26

GOBLIN'S STONE, TESS AND ME

It didn't matter that the next morning I had woken up with the full stop beside me – I had also woken up with a heart full of gratitude. The massage hadn't removed my writer's block, but I was moved; moved by the kindness shown to me by someone who I hadn't known for long.

Things moved fluidly here: words, animals, people, kindness. It was as if the open space of the countryside allowed things to breathe and exist more freely. By contrast, the buildings of the city and their high concrete walls not just housed people but feelings, turning buildings into hothouses filled with emotions that never felt quite free enough to be expressed. It added to the pollution of the city.

I hadn't long had breakfast when there was a phone call from Tess, Andrew's wife from across the valley. She was also a gardener and had an impressive polytunnel where she grew aubergines, courgettes, garlic and all the things that I thought would never grow in Wales.

'Hello, Lovely!' She was always so sunny.

'Hello, Tess.'

'I have the afternoon off and wanted to see if you'd like to go to the cairn near Goblin's Stone – if you're still struggling with writing? It will do you the world of good. And with this wind, it will definitely blow the cobwebs away!'

Goblin's Stone was only a mile up the road, the local colloquial name given to the Bronze Age/Roman site. Near Goblin's Stone was a cairn that stood on top of a mountain at 415 metres. I had never been to the cairn near Goblin's Stone, even though it was only down the road from The Long Barn.

Tess arrived in her old red jeep and beeped the horn to alert me to her arrival. I looked out of the window and saw her waving enthusiastically. It was impossible not to feel positive with her around. She was sensitive, joyful and good. Life wasn't a puzzle for her, as it was for so many; it was just meant to be lived. There was a real simplicity to Tess that made me feel safe. There are some people in life who you know would do you good if you spent more time with them. She was one of those people. I jumped into her jeep and we whizzed off with the wind behind us, in the hope that there was alchemy in nature.

It wasn't a long walk to the cairn; we had parked at the bottom of the hill, not far from the Roman road. We jumped over a country gate and walked up a narrow grassy track. The wind was already crashing about around our ears, but we persevered and pushed against it. I imagined the wind I was walking against was the breeze-block full stop. I felt a small triumph as I clenched my fists and took Herculean steps to reach the cairn at the top of the mountain. I had a job to do; walls to abseil and barriers to break.

'I always come here when I need some space!' Tess shouted. Even though we walked side by side, we had started to shout our conversation as the wind got louder.

We stopped walking along the side of the path and took to climbing up the mountain to reach the cairn. The merciless wind pushed us back and willed us to turn around. But we didn't; we laughed and squealed in delight as our coats and woolly hats turned inside out. And we laughed at the sheer lunacy of walking to a high point in a wind that was so wilful. We fought the wind like the Romans that once walked this very terrain.

By the time we reached the cairn, a mound of stones thought to signify a Bronze Age burial ground, it was almost impossible to hear each other. The wind was so strong, our words were snatched from our mouths as soon as they were uttered, then got lost in the vortex. Tess and I gave out voiceless screams as the wind swallowed us whole. We lifted our arms, surrendering to the forces of nature, ready to be transported. It was why we were there: to give ourselves to something that was bigger than us. We stumbled around, twisting and turning like the autumn leaves, drunk on life. The wind was so powerful, we leant back and the force of it propped us up and turned us into puppets: we were windsurfing. I had never felt an invisible force so powerful. My long hair slapped my face and covered my eyes. Tess walked around the cairn, the subject of our pilgrimage, as if she was being pulled in the opposite direction by wild horses. And in a way, she was; the wind took on many guises that month in autumn. I wasn't as strong as Tess, and it took me longer to walk around the cairn. I had never dealt with a force so hell-bent on preventing me from moving forward – except grief. A small child would have easily been blown away. There had been winds here so powerful they had lifted lambs and sheep into the air. Tess and I were no different from all the other animals that were out in the wilderness that day. We felt fearless, and wild.

'We're so lucky to be here!' Tess yelled, a yell that managed to escape the vortex, a yell that reached my ears. She was making the most of windsurfing; she swapped between leaning back and leaning forward. And whatever way she leant, she was held up by the wind like a pair bookends holding together all the stories of her life. I took her lead and did the same, leaning back and then forward. The wind sucked on my face, distorting it.

I stopped windsurfing and tried to take control of the movements of my body. I looked around me, taking in the panoramic view. On the side of the cairn was a dense forest. It looked mythical and magical, perhaps the home of fairies and goblins. This was *The Lord of The Rings* territory. Standing on top of the mountain, feeling a force that I had never felt before, I would have believed anything. I allowed the wind to spin me around, take me somewhere, anywhere. I could see the western edge of the Brecon Beacons to the east of me. To the north was Snowdonia. And then there was the faint line of the sea of Cardigan Bay.

Tess managed to sit on one of the rocks on the cairn and attempted to take pictures with her phone, then quickly put it back in her pocket as the wind tried to snatch it. I started to windsurf again, and after a few minutes, Tess joined me. We stood opposite each other and windsurfed like ten-year-old girls. The wind took our screams and carried them out to sea. We were both warriors, out in the wilds, curious and free.

Briefly, for just a moment, we forgot the presence of Romans and all that had been before us. It was just us: Tess and me. This mountain was ours and from this high point, where everything looked small, we ruled this little part of the world. We had fought for the right to be here; we were the conquerors of mountains. And when the wind entered our mouths as we screamed, we welcomed it. We could taste all that we were a part of: trees, animals, sea. We were everything.

When we had had enough of giving ourselves up to the forces of nature, we walked back down to the narrow and grassy path. We were thrill-seekers who had dared to dance in the wind and claim the heart of a beast. But the heart that we claimed wasn't a beast's; it was our own hearts. We were buoyant and laughed, not at anything particular, just at the peculiarities of life. We reached the bottom of the mountain and slipped back into the quietude of the countryside.

27

HARA THE SOUND HEALER

'Hara said that I should take you over to hers. She thinks she might have something for you,' Tess said as she put in the key in the ignition.

'That's nice of her.'

'She's concerned about you. I spoke to her just before I picked you up. Maybe she can help too? She seems to think she can.'

'Are you free now – you don't need to go home, do you?' I asked.

'No, I'm free. Shall we see if she's in, Lovely?'

'Yes, let's go.'

We zoomed off again in the red jeep in a bubble of hope.

I had never been to Hara's house and I hadn't seen much of her since the summer party at Caer Cadwgan. She was always so busy, wild swimming and putting on her dance classes, and of course having people visit her for sound healing. But I could imagine her home quite easily: lots of colour and things of her creation scattered about the house. Some people's domestic environments could be imagined without much thought, because those people could only live and thrive in particular spaces. To exist outside those imagined parameters would be akin to colouring outside the lines of a drawing. I had once envied the certainty of such lives; the sense of belonging that was instilled in them. But I was realising that life was more of an abstract painting than a colour-by-numbers canvas. I was surprised how this realisation had only just crept up on me. I had been colouring outside the lines of conformity my whole life.

We pulled into Hara's drive. Her house was a beautiful peach-coloured cottage with green painted windows. A host of old motorbikes and other ageing vehicles stood outside. Si, Hara's husband, was a motorcycle enthusiast. He liked pulling things apart and then putting them back together again.

Hara opened the door; she had heard the jeep pull in. 'Hello, ladies! Come in before you get blown away!!' She left the front door open and we entered the house and walked straight into the kitchen. I quickly closed the door behind me, shutting out the autumn leaves. And there she stood, Hara, in the environment that was unashamedly Hara. The kitchen dripped with purples, greens and oranges. A farmhouse table sat in the middle of this chaos of colour. And the table was full of all sorts of things that told a story of a full life. In children's books, houses are painted in outlandish colours; an exaggeration of real life, a fantasy. But this was Hara's house; a reality, yet a house that belonged in a children's book. Old copper pots hung from the ceiling, and there was stuff everywhere: plant pots, dishes, paintings, sculptures, jars of pickles; empty jars and cutlery and pictures. It was a house that was alive with a sense of living and doing.

Tess and I removed the things that were on the kitchen chairs so that we could sit down, while Hara busied herself with making tea. I was too engrossed looking around Hara's kitchen to notice that she was trying to talk to me. I felt I had dropped into a fantasy world of colour. The young girl in me asked me to look for a jar containing the eyes of newts and the poisoned heart of a dragon. It was certain to be here in this children's fantasy house.

'Here, something I made. It's a new version of the mint chocolate ganache. I've used a different liqueur. Go ahead, taste it.'

She pushed the dessert that sat in a large glass container towards us and then struggled to find two clean spoons. 'Here, let me wash these two,' she said as she found a couple of teaspoons lying on the table. Tess took hold of the teaspoon. 'Hara never makes ordinary food; it's always special food.' And she was right. We both greedily sucked on the teaspoons long after we had tasted the dessert.

'Kiran, why didn't you tell me about your writer's block? It was Sophie who told me. You know I'd have something for you.' She sounded disappointed and I felt a pang of guilt, as if I had kept a secret, when I hadn't. 'You know I do sound healing. I am happy to give you a session.'

'That's so kind of you; it's just writer's block, that's all. It usually just goes away, but . . .'

'That's what sound healing does – it removes blockages.'

'Well, at this stage, I'll try anything – it's become almost painful.'

Tess got up to go home so that Hara could get on with the sound healing, and on her way out, she gave me a reassuring hug. 'You'll be OK, Lovely – Hara will sort you out. She's helped me before.'

Hara was the third person in the valley who was trying to help me with my drought of words. I'm not sure how news spread so quickly, even news that wasn't really news, just everyday living, like my writer's block. I imagined it was the ferocious autumnal wind that swept our inner thoughts and struggles into the homes and ears of others.

'Come with me. I'll take you to the therapy room.' Hara said.

We walked through into the living room where we passed a lime green piano. I couldn't just quickly walk through; I needed to stop and take in the view. Large patchwork cushions sat on a purple sofa. Hara had made these herself; she was a brilliant seamstress. On the mantelpiece was a beautiful green carriage clock adorned with pink roses. I stood and stared at it. Hara had created it herself using découpage, the art of decorating an object by gluing on paper cutouts and adding special paint effects, gold leaf and other decorative elements. Hara proudly pointed out all the other wonderful things she had created, like a tour guide in an art gallery. I suddenly thought about Donna and Jane and so many others that lived in the valley – they were all so creative. Maybe that's what happened in the countryside; without the distraction that the towns and cities had, people turned in on themselves and connected with their creative side. It made me think of the days before TV and radio, when people sat around a fire telling stories, sewing or playing the piano.

The small therapy room was like all the other rooms, filled with things and objects. Hara took down notes as I positioned myself on her therapy table. I lay on my back, my feet on puffed-up cushions. I closed my eyes and could feel her hands hovering above me, assessing my auric field and the energy centres, known as chakras. She started to make vocal sounds, not words but the sounds of vowels. Before the session began, she had said she would be using her voice and hands to search for imbalances or blockages, old wounds or negative experiences imprinted on the energy field. Working through the chakras, she would rebalance and give healing where necessary. Right by my ears I could hear a rattling and then the sound of a drum. I was happy to be oblivious to the workings and the methods of it all; I wanted to feel my way through it, like one would a poem. The rattling and the drumming felt tribal and I willed all the little parts of me that lay dormant to wake up.

And then there was silence.

The silence weighed on me like a heavy duvet in the height of summer. It muffled sound and restricted my movement. The countryside had started to feel the same: too quiet and provincial. It mirrored my internal silence that started to gnaw inside of me. Because of that silence, I couldn't cope with the idea of it being silent outside of me too; in the valley, in the sound healing, the whole world became silent. Bring back the bells, the drums, the chatter of people, the 'mind the gap' announcements and the howling wind.

My body moved and wriggled; the silence taunted me. I was restless. I stretched my legs, pointed my toes, my arms reached out to the ceiling. My head turned to the left and then to the right. I took deep breaths and then yawned. I needed to be on my side, my body willed me to lie on my side, to turn away from it all. I would never have thought that silence could be so disturbing.

The sounds came back and I was no longer alone. It felt like Hara was back in the room, even though she never left. The sounds of the drums and rattle vibrated around the room as if they too were restless. Hara's hands hovered above me again until they reached my feet, then she pressed them down, as if to keep me rooted and not to fly off to some other dimension.

After the session I felt dazed and needed a drink of water. I'm not sure what had happened, but something had. Hara talked me through the hour-long session and the chakras. My 'root' she said was 'muddy' and 'fuzzy', but 'strong'. As for my 'sacral', the chakra that rules creativity and survival emotions: 'Your energy here was all over the place and needed clearing and brightening. It was heavy and dull, but very active.' She carried on with her list of findings of the chakras, like a shopping list. 'Your solar plexus was strong and clear, but there's a clear knock to your confidence. Your solar energy is very powerful.' Then there was my 'heart', and she rested into herself and took a sigh. 'Connecting to your heart was like the opening and unfolding of many petals of a lotus; very open and full, lots of giving and movement.' And for the 'brow': 'There was something you don't want to see or look at, a closing off of a perception evident here. Also, something unresolved to do with your mother.'

The sentence was left hanging in the air. I hadn't really spoken to Hara about my mother much. But I wasn't surprised at what she said. I was amazed at the capacity the human body has to house so much pain. But all I could say was: 'Thank you, Hara.' And then walked back home.

28

THE RAMS AND THE EWES

Autumn meant I saw fewer people outdoors; people tended to stay indoors more as the nights drew in. They started to hibernate like the animals. It was a time when people no longer left their doors wide open; it was a time for shutting the world out and a time for preservation. This made me feel lonely. I was used to walking in city crowds. The only things that walked together here in a collective bubble were the sheep. So I yearned for London and the snippets of conversation I would hear walking in the streets. I lived vicariously in sentences that weren't even aimed at me. People around here didn't like London. I remembered Wilf's comment about my home city: it's best avoided. Rod, Glen and Sarah also had little time for London. For them, the city was cold and steely; a place where human warmth was lacking. But for me, it was the autumn of the countryside that made me feel a sense of isolation. In the city, I was in a library of people, surrounded by the stories of the lives of others. And the people I chose to befriend were books I chose to take off the shelf. How could London be lonely?

Just as spring had a flurry of excitement about it due to lambing, the autumn brought in a second wave of excitement in the world of sheep: mating. As the evenings got shorter, ewes and rams mated in a process called tupping. Many considered this as the beginning of the lambing year. A tup, also known as a ram, a male sheep, would be introduced to a field of ewes in the autumn so that there would be lambs in the season of spring.

'How's the writer's block now?' Grenville asked. He was not just our builder, he was now someone we considered a friend. He was back at The Long Barn fixing the cupboard under the stairs. He was on a break and we both sat in the kitchen drinking coffee. I told him about the massage, Goblin's Stone and the sound healing; all unexpected gifts. 'I definitely felt something shift in the sound healing and walking up the cairn, though I couldn't tell you what.'

Simon did say that, after seeing Hara, I was in a far more buoyant mood. But something else happened that shifted the block: tupping season. Once again, there was activity in the hills and the mountains. It lifted the sleepy countryside lull that hung in the air like the morning mist of the valley. I had got lost in those tiny droplets of water that were suspended in the air, which had slowed me down with their misty lullaby. The season of closing down had made me feel listless and I had succumbed to its ennui. But it was now tupping season, the start of lambing.

The excitement of possibilities of new life put an end to my stupor.

'You know it's a good ol' ram that is,' Grenville said as he looked out of our kitchen window. Through our kitchen window we saw the full circle of life: lambs being born, then getting older, the separation of the lambs from the ewes and now the very beginnings of life. 'Last year, in Ireland, a ram was sold for over £37k. Yes, you could get a lot of money for a good ram . . .'

I was shocked: 'Bloody hell, really?' I spluttered.

'Yes, but only a small number of farmers around here can afford to pay that kind of money.'

One afternoon, a few days ago, I had looked out of the window and noticed there were two rams in the field of around a hundred sheep. I had still not worked out the different breeds of sheep, but even with my limited knowledge, I could tell the difference between the rams and the ewes. The rams were stocky, thick-necked bruisers with huge testicles that now dominated the field. The idyllic pastoral scene was now running high on hormones. The rams walked around with their heads up, noses in the air with curled top lips, smelling fertile ewes. The breed of ram was Texel – a really strange-looking animal with a squarish, boxish, dog-like face. I had never seen sheep that looked so much like dogs. Everything seemed to go on through our south-facing windows; they told the story of life.

Even before the rams were put in with the ewes, farmers were matchmaking, carefully pairing their ewes and rams to create the best offspring possible. There was a saying: 'Guy Fawkes ram, April fool lamb'. If you put the ram into the field in November, expect the lambs end of March and early April. Pregnancy in ewes lasts four to five months and, unlike some other animals, ewes only come into season once a year. There is only a small window of possibilities.

'It's all about breeding you see, so some farmers, if they can, mind you, will spend big money on rams,' Grenville said as he put his empty coffee mug down. 'You see the green-coloured dye on the back of the ewes?'

'Yes,' I responded.

'Well, that's from the ram. The ram has a dye on his underside, so when mating occurs, the ram leaves his mark . . .'

'Ah! This I know!' I explained. I was happy to declare that I had taken notice of the green colour that had suddenly appeared on many of the ewes.

'Good! Good!' Grenville said as he nodded enthusiastically. 'There are so many things that make a good ram, Kiran. A ram must have good feet. It will need to get around a field quite bit to service those ewes. It needs to be properly mobile you see. Then the teeth – if it doesn't have good teeth, it's not eating properly, so not healthy. And then there's . . .'

Before he could finish, his mobile rang. He waved me off and walked to the job he was there for while he spoke on the phone. I learnt a lot from Grenville. He was always so willing and enthusiastic about telling me about Wales, the people in it and the farming way of life. Grenville was a proud Welshman and I could tell he enjoyed the fact that I was inquisitive about the area that he had grown up in. He was a strong-looking man and he always walked around with a pencil tucked behind his ear. This was his land; the playground of his youth. He sometimes said things like: 'I'm glad you're enjoying it here' with a broad smile. But I'd be lying if I said I always felt happy in my new abode.

The quietude of the country was a catalyst to thoughts that had been long forgotten. Self-examination can feel terrible, but at times, it can soften edges that were once too sharp to touch. So I tried to settle into this life and my new way of being, even on those days I wished I were in an exhibition in a London gallery. And on those days, I'd look out at the pastoral scene from my window and remember that landscapes similar to this one had been painted by artists and were now housed in a gallery in London. There is nothing more generous than a window.

WINTER

29

THE SECRET HIGHLANDS

The Highland cattle looked beautiful. I was driving past the cattle grid at the top of the Roman road and stopped the car. I could never just drive past the Highlands. Just as Wilf wished people would step out of their cars to hear the cuckoo, I thought the same about the Highland cattle. There are some things in life that rightfully demanded our attention.

Eight Highlands lived on the higher ground of the mountains. They came in rich colours of copper, blonde and black. I wasn't sure whether it was characteristic of the breed or just these eight cows, but they seemed gentler than the other, regular cattle. We had dairy Friesian cows, Guernsey and Jersey cows in their caramel coats scattered around the valley. I saw these breeds often dotted about everywhere. And sometimes they would be at the back of our house, when Dai would put in his cattle instead of sheep. These ubiquitous breeds stayed in the lower parts of the valley; it was just the Highland cattle that lived on the higher parts of the mountain in the area. Sarah told me that the Highland cows didn't give as much milk as the other cows. One Highland could produce on average around 2 gallons of milk per day, compared to 6 for a Jersey cow. But their milk had a high butterfat content, which was great for making butter and cheese.

Perhaps it was their heavy fringes that made these Highland cattle seem more docile and coy? They reminded me of mammoths with their long hair and horns; they gave off an air of majesty.

Making my way home from the shops, I decided to take the longer route. It was the first day of December and in the supermarket pyramids of brilliantly wrapped Christmas puddings were being thrown at shoppers like friendly hand grenades. Advent calendars were on full display. For years, on the first day of December, Simon would always buy me an advent calendar. But that had stopped, like so many other things. An advent calendar now was a countdown to my mother's death. So, instead of opening the window of an advent calendar that revealed cheap chocolate, I drove to the higher part of the valley, opened a different type of window and let the Highlands in.

I always got out of the car to greet the Highlands. They weren't as skittish as the other cattle; they moved slower and didn't seem to mind me being there. In fact, they often walked towards me as if to greet me; they recognised me now. A rusty Highland walked in my direction in a bovine sluggish way. 'Hello, Highland.' I always chatted to these 'Hairy Coos', as some people called them.

December wind wrapped itself around my neck like an unfriendly scarf, reminding me that it was time to start wearing one. It was always a little bit windier and wilder up here. It was easy to forget that the valley was populated with people when I stood on this part of the land; I could really feel my solitariness, an erratic wind and roaming beasts my only company. I wasn't afraid of it. Growing up with an alcoholic father, there was a lot of fighting and shouting, so I learnt very early on in life that silence was golden. As a child, like a locket, I kept silence in my heart; it wasn't a boring place but a safe place. There was something sacred about silence. Thomas Aquinas, a theologian and philosopher who lived in the Middle Ages, fell into a deep silence. He had taken a glimpse of life in its ineffable glory; an inexpressible mystery that could not be voiced by words, that silenced him. I understood this so much more now: the world is bigger than our minds.

'I bet you look beautiful when it snows.' Just as I said those words to the copper Highland, I decided, if it snowed, I would come here and take photos of the Highlands and make cards out of them. I had stopped sending cards when Christmas changed for me, but before that, I would often make my own seasonal cards. Now, instead of sending Christmas cards, I sent letters to friends. This felt more appropriate for the Christmas that belonged to me now.

I was behind a low stone wall, only the distance of a few feet between me and the eight Highlands. I could hear them breathe, deeply and purposefully. I liked to think that they too could hear me breathe, and the idea felt comforting. The mesh between the animal world and my world pierced by the sharp edges of our crystallised winter breath. In this way, our worlds were made closer; the distance and difference between us was made smaller. We occupied the same world and breathed life into one another. 'When the heavy mist and fog starts, I'll come up and see you again. I'd really like that.'

When I was a child of 11 and 12, every Friday I would arrive home from school before anyone else. My school finished at 3pm and my elder two siblings would finish at 3.30pm. My mother and father would still be at work. And when I arrived home from school to an empty house, I would drop my school bag off and visit a lone horse. My house was near a park with a small field and that's where the horse lived. I would take an apple from the fruit bowl to feed it. I would tell the horse about my day at school and who fell out with whom. Although I told my siblings and parents about the horse, no one had seen it or bothered to visit it. It felt like a delicious secret to me; me and the secret horse with our secret conversations. And this is how I felt when I went to visit the Highlands. I was a girl of 12.

I heard a car pull up. I had never seen a passer-by in all the times I had visited the Highland cattle. I felt slightly irked. This was my secret place – I didn't want to share the Highlands. A lady who looked like she was in her fifties came out of the car and picked up some eggs displayed by the nearby farm. She dropped some coins in the honesty box. She waved at me, 'Hi there!' I waved back in politeness. I was enjoying the still place I held with the Highlands. The utterance of the stranger's words contaminated the wild silence. I was never misanthropic, but it was the beginning of December and I wanted to be left alone. I was selective about who I invited in; the advent calendar I opened now had fewer windows. I was at odds with the day and human conversation wore me out. I was seeking solace in the worldless communication of animals.

'They're beautiful, aren't they?' The lady now stood beside me. She wore a pleated floral skirt with green wellies and a navy Barbour jacket. She looked more polished than the people around here; rather glamorous.

'Yes, they're wonderful,' I said as I turned to stare at the Highlands again.

I didn't want her to be here with me, a stranger witnessing my strangeness. I was feeling fragile like I knew I would on this day. Like I always did on this day, the first day of December, the beginning of the end of my mother's life. I was afraid that the wrong words from someone could break my thin skin and release a lava of pain. A small tug on a thread of regret can unravel a whole a garment. Communication with humans was arduous and awkward. Words felt unnecessary; unwanted; insignificant. I needed to be silent. The forced communication with this stranger made me feel how ill-prepared I was for the new month. Without her presence, I wouldn't have noticed. I would have sleepwalked through the day in a protected bubble, imperceptibly, unnoticed by others: a living ghost.

'They're very hardy. They originated in the Scottish

Highlands and the Outer Hebrides islands of Scotland.' The lady was now sharing the stone wall with me, her arms folded, resting on the stone wall, mirroring me.

'I like spending time with them. They make me feel happy.' I prised the words out of mouth, pushing them out before they disappeared.

'They make me happy too. I often come here with my flask of tea,' the stranger said.

This special place, the higher part of the valley, the Highland cattle, didn't just belong to me, they belonged to her too. It was easy for me to believe they were my own secret herd – I had never spoken or seen anyone else here. It was a childish fanciful notion laced with the childhood romance of keeping secrets.

I was about to ask the stranger if she knew who owned the cattle and then stopped myself. It was an unimportant detail that would get in the way of my special moments with them; debasing them with ideas of ownership and money, man and beast. I liked to think of them as free-roaming animals and enjoyed thinking about them when I sat by the fire in The Long Barn. Come snow, wind, hail or rain, the Highlands stood firm as they had for hundreds of years.

The stranger offered me tea. This suggestion had surprised me; I didn't want tea, but it seemed churlish to say no to a stranger's offer. The stranger came back with a floral flask and two red plastic cups. I imagined her in the summer, a wicker picnic basket, her hair in a scarf and her face held up to the sun, like a satellite facing the Earth. 'Here we go.' She handed me a cup and carefully poured the tea. And then we both looked at each other, her eyes kind, bright, blue.

We resumed our positions on the stone wall, this time with our hands wrapped around red plastic cups.

'You know, Queen Victoria is said to have commented on a trip to the Highlands that she preferred the red-coloured cattle to all the other colours. Everyone tried to please the Queen, of course, and this resulted in selective breeding, with the colour black gradually declining.'

I didn't know what to say; I had nothing to offer except my pensiveness.

'But I think you look very grand, Bertie!!' She was talking to the black Highland.

'Have you named all of the eight cattle?' I asked.

'Oh yes! That rusty one there is Gertie. Blondie is Alfred. The copper is Hector . . .'

I don't know what it was, maybe the hot tea or the fact that she had named all the cattle, but my icy exterior thawed and I no longer feared the breaking of my skin.

Under a grey-blue, marbled, cold sky, the stranger and I laughed at the chosen names of the animals that weren't ours. I had never given the Highlands names. Naming them would mean trapping them in a sort of possession; throwing a ring of a lasso over their heads; making them less wild and free.

Propped up against the stone wall, we both shared the Highland cattle view of my advent calendar window. It was the first time in years that I had made space for something other than my grief during the month of December. And I was glad. The stranger demanded nothing of me except company. There were no demands for me to feign happiness. The stranger told me that the collective name for Highland cattle is a 'fold' and not a 'herd', as is the usual collective noun for cows. They have a double coat; the outer coat covers a downy undercoat. The outside coat is oily and long so that snow and sleet can easily slip off. The long fringes help to keep the snow and sleet away from their eyes, and in the summer, they keep the flies away.

'Highland cattle have been living alongside people for thousands of years. In the winter, the cows would come into the home; their body heat helped warm homes.' I immediately thought of Gwylyn and Tegwyn, the elderly brother and sister who once lived in the decrepit house down the road in the 1990s. They would bring in their sheep in the winter to keep warm.

The stranger and I were almost huddled together, and she now spoke in hushed tones as if she were hosting a nature programme. We spent precious time marvelling at the cattle. Neither of us had introduced ourselves. Our names didn't matter; it was just the Highland cattle that had names, they took precedence. We were nameless visitors and admirers who stood in awe.

30

THE VERY FOGGY DAY

A few days after my encounter with the stranger, I decided to do one of my long walks. It was 1pm and the small scope of daylight already felt like it was dimming. I passed Wilf's shed and saw light pouring out of the open door. It drew me in, like a moth. In winter, like the animals, I was drawn to warm places. I walked in and there was Wilf, huffing and puffing on a chair, trying to put on new wellies.

'Oh, crikey! You made me jump!' he cried.

I stood and giggled. 'I'm sorry, the door's wide open.'

'I think they are maybe too small,' he said, his face red with exasperation. 'The lady said they were my size.' I stood and stared – he was determined to have a fight with the wellies. For a moment I wondered whether I should help him. I could hold a welly while he stood, holding onto my shoulder for balance, as he placed one foot in at a time. Would that work?

'Oh dear, I will just have to return these boots. I bought them from a shop in Aberystwyth.' Just as he said this, his feet, which were clearly too big for the wellies, squeezed into the new footwear. He took a deep breath and rested into himself and sighed. His face lit up in appreciation of small victories.

'What makes a good farmer is that he likes the job that he's doing,' he said as he stood up awkwardly and steadied himself, the wellies evidently too small. He started to walk around his shed, his facial expressions giving away the ill-fitting footwear.

'Most people work eight to five, isn't it? And they're always looking at the clock. When it's time to finish, I never look at my watch,' Wilf said. I looked around his shed. There were signs of his favourite meal – fish paste, a loaf of bread and a large onion – along with a box of porridge oats and a half-empty packet of grapes. But there was no clock. And I had never seen him with a wristwatch. The shed was a place that existed outside time and space. But that wasn't entirely true. Wilf didn't watch the clock, but he did watch his surroundings; the change of colour and temperature of his environment. He knew it was time for the cuckoo to arrive and the time for it to leave; the time for the earth to wake and the time for dormancy. I now knew enough about farming to know there was a time for tupping, lambing, shearing and for separating the ewes from the lambs. Time wasn't a man-made constraint on his day – it was nature's.

An apron with the Welsh flag, a pair of colourful socks and a plaid shirt hung neatly on a clothes horse outside the shed door. It had rained and the items were soaking. A washing machine stood in between water containers and sheep feed; more home than shed.

Wilf walked over to his little office space, collected his green waterproofs and started to put them on. 'I am looking forward to getting on my tractor now. I've been looking forward to it since I got up this morning.' A seven-year-old Wilf could have spoken that very sentence. It made me smile – not many people announced the simple pleasures in their day; usually they went unnoticed. I immediately thought of the small joys I had that morning: a completed difficult crossword and a delicious breakfast of bacon and eggs. I thought of Schopenhauer's quote that I had only read the other day:

> Just as we do not feel the health of our whole body, but only the small spot where the shoe pinches, so we do not think of all our affairs that are going on perfectly well, but only of some insignificant trifle that annoys us.

Wilf celebrated his joy of riding a tractor. The pinch of his wellies; a minor detail in his day.

Wilf walked out of the shed and I followed, ready to take the road and brave the cold.

'Crikey, it covers some area, doesn't it?' Wilf shouted.

Wilf was looking at the huge tree just by his shed. Strangely, I had never really noticed it or looked at it, but we both stood and stared at its magnificence: a tree that was rooted and free. It was free because it had avoided the chainsaw and was allowed to flourish and reach its full potential. Like the tree, if people fulfilled their purpose in life, and were authentic, I believed they had freedom. It was why Wilf never looked at the clock. Farming wasn't his job – it was his life.

In the distance, behind Wilf's shed, was a forest. For some reason, we both chose to stare out to it, swallowing and digesting our surroundings; allowing nature to centre us. The gnarly bare winter trees looked like pleading hands that searched for the sky, the covert stars and the moon. A fog started to envelope us. Sometimes, in the winter, the mist and fog never lifted. It hung around; a house guest that never left.

'Perhaps I'll get on the tractor tomorrow, once the fog has gone.' The fog was suddenly so heavy, it was difficult to see five feet ahead. I followed Wilf indoors.

The fog was so intense now. I considered walking back home.

Wilf started to remove his waterproof jacket. Instead of having a button at the top where his neck was, he closed the neck of his jacket with a clothes peg. And his plaid shirt had the collar rather crudely removed. It was the same for the shirt that was hanging up on the clothes horse. In actual fact, all his shirts had their collars removed. He was a man of practicalities; he wasn't going to wear a tie to feed the sheep – it was superfluous to requirements.

'I will be going out for my walk later this evening, like I always do. I get all my thinking done then, you see.' It was true, Wilf walked every evening – whatever the weather. Driving back from work, Sarah would often pass him. She would complain because in the dark she sometimes never saw Wilf and was sure that one day she would run him over. She would see him walking with his two walking sticks oblivious to her approaching car. He never carried a torch or wore any high-visibility clothes. He walked in the dark. Sarah was grateful when the long days arrived and Wilf was visible to her again. And then she would wind her window down and yell: 'Hello!'

'The only time I stopped walking was when I had a stroke. A year ago I could hardly move, you see. I remember them moving me from one bed to the next – it was agony. I didn't believe I'd ever be well again . . .'

His voice broke and trailed off into the far-off distance where he kept his memories alive. He sat on his chair again. The force of the memory of the stroke was too overwhelming to bear standing up; it crushed him like a wave. And there was nothing he could do but surrender to it – we can't ride out all the waves in our lives.

'I wanted to go back to the sheep . . .'

The end of his sentence broke off again. He wiped tears that flowed like a determined river with the palms of his hands. He was reminded of the vulnerability of his existence, how his everyday quiet joys of living could be taken away: a simple walk in his valley, the feeding of the sheep that needed him the same way that he needed them. He didn't ask for much in his life: the freedom to feed his beloved sheep and the freedom to walk his beloved valley. But he was remembering a time when these simple everyday joys were facing extinction. Who was he without his valley, without his sheep?

'Wilf, you're perfectly well now. You have your sheep.'

'I couldn't cope staying in bed all those days. I watched David Attenborough on television. That's the only thing that kept me going, and the sheep. The sheep helped me – I knew they were relying on me to get better.'

Talking about David Attenborough stopped Wilf's tears; Attenborough made life magic again.

'If I could go anywhere, it would be the Great Wall of China – I would love to see it. The amount of work that must have gone into making it must be unbelievable. Perhaps it took a century, I don't know. All I know is that I will never walk it.'

My heart swelled and then broke knowing Wilf would never make it to the Great Wall of China, or meet David Attenborough. My body felt heavy from acknowledging the unfairness of life.

'When I go for my walk, from the top of the valley, I can see the sheep from the top road. I can see the sun going down in the west. I can see the trees and the hills and the little rivers. Everything looks so small and so far away. I don't know if anybody else would see it like that. Everything is so perfect. And I feel like I'm on the top of the world.'

I changed my mind; I would go for my walk. I bid Wilf farewell.

As I walked, the fog accompanied me; it held me still in its icy embrace. One day, I thought to myself, I would take Wilf's route, but in the meantime, I was still working out my own.

I reached the top of the Roman road and stopped and turned around. From this slightly elevated position, I could look down on the fog that covered the fields. For a moment I felt I was a part of a Victorian novel. The already quiet countryside was made even quieter by the weight of the fog.

I turned the corner and followed the road. The bushes and the boulders on the side of the road that I was so used to seeing had almost disappeared in the fog. I wasn't frightened by the disappearance of landmarks – I had learnt to embrace the wanderer in me.

A few brave birds, not afraid of freezing mid-flight, chased each other in the grey sky.

I could hear that there were sheep in the fields, yet I couldn't see them. But every so often, the cloud-like woolly body of a sheep would be revealed by popping out from a cloud of fog. A cloud falling out of a cloud – how funny.

A sheep's face popped out close to the fence, the rest of its body lost in fog. It startled me, a bodiless sheep. My walk became a walk of reveals. I felt a sense of freedom walking in this unmapped terrain that the fog had created. I was a little lost, but that was OK. One must get lost in life every so often; how else are we to find ourselves in uncharted territory? I was beginning to realise that too much emphasis is put on finding one's place in life, and not enough importance on the teachings of being lost. I had lost my immediate family and I had severed links with those who didn't show me love. To them, I was an abstract painting: nonsensical. But I had become the double-rooted carrot in my garden, navigating my way around rocks and stones and flourishing anyway. In the density of the December fog, a fog that was shapeless and concealed a well-trodden path,

I walked free. Some blood relationships felt like a form of locked-in syndrome; a stunting of personal growth. There was only one thing left to do: redefine family. It had become obvious to me that the best gift anyone could give to someone was to show them their true potential, and then to let them swim in it.

31

THE GHOSTS OF CHRISTMAS PAST

On Christmas Day 2011, two years before my mother was diagnosed, my mum, dad and sister (who lived with them) called me at 8am. We always called each other on Christmas Day morning. We had all opened our presents and I spoke to all three of them. We wished each other a merry Christmas and thanked each other for the gifts. Dad told me I had given him the best present – a framed photo of him and his cousin. Mum and Dad went to church for the morning service and then spent the afternoon in church having Christmas lunch with the Indian Christian community, coming over to my house later that evening. My sister and cousins came for lunch cooked by Simon and me. We loved hosting Christmas. I was happy – we were finally having the peaceful Christmases other families had, unlike previous years when alcohol would ruin everything. I carried the pain of those days for many years. But I had finally, almost, let go of them.

In those first few Decembers after my mother's death, Christmas was something I flinched away from like an injection: I knew it would hurt. I'd walk out of shops, suffocated by tinsel and baubles. And I couldn't understand how, on the first anniversary of my mother's death, people could send me Christmas cards that wished me joy and happiness; seeds planted in an arid land. I still chose to put up a Christmas tree in my house. I liked sitting on the floor by it, guarding it as if it were a memory that was trying to run away. I'd spend many evenings sitting next to it, remembering Christmas past.

Back in Wales, the smell of Christmas filled Donna's kitchen. She had asked me to join her in an afternoon of arts and crafts, and we were making Christmas wreaths.

In the town the Christmas lights were up. Shop windows had posters advertising the season's fair. But the brown and green winter landscape of the countryside was free from the twinkle of artificial lights.

'What I've done is put this orange zest oil in the wreaths,' Donna said. 'Here, take some home – you can do the same in your house. Put it in your potpourri.'

I looked outside the kitchen window. The short span of daylight was still present, but only just. I stared out to the undulating hills and imagined they were protecting me from the onslaught of Christmas, just like the Roman signal station here that had once protected someone. I needed to feel protected, despite knowing that the trick to life was to embrace it, even if I could no longer stomach it.

'Come over on Christmas Day in the evening. It will be nice to have a drink with a few adults.'

I liked how casual Christmas was out here in the country. There was less pressure for it to be a five-star occasion: London was a five-star city. When I had wished Happy Easter to Dai, he said: 'It's the same as any other day, isn't it?' Maybe, through osmosis, living in an agricultural environment rooted you to the earth, so people didn't jump on the merry-go-round of what was temporary? Few things in life take precedence over toiling the earth.

Donna made us both a cup of coffee. Simon was at home playing with Blackberry. She was around 11 weeks old, still too tiny to be let out; there was a good chance a bird of prey would take her away. The sound of children watching TV drifted into the kitchen. 'Remember to tell Andy if you'd like the pork too. The turkeys are almost all taken now.' As with most of our friends, we ordered our turkey from Donna and Andy's smallholding. And the pork was from their own pigs. I liked the fact that Glen and Rod and Tess and Andrew were also getting their meat from Donna and Andy. Caer Cadwgan was looking after us all; an invisible thread that kept us together.

In the Christmases following my mother's death, I spent Christmas Day with very few people. Christmas was now a sombre affair, more 'In the Bleak Midwinter' than 'Rockin' Around The Christmas Tree'. In London, I felt uncomfortable telling people this. At this time of year, you are measured as a person according to how much you celebrate. There is a pressure to go large, be big, be bold, spend all your cash, invite as many people as you can and take up all the space that's available to you. It's the behaviour of frightened animals; making themselves appear larger than they really are. Perhaps city people were afraid to be small and feel insignificant? The philosopher David Hume said: 'The life of man is of no greater importance to the universe than that of an oyster.' I now occupied a small space in the world, just a corner. The city bravado did not suit me. So I lied. I pretended that I was having a Christmas full of frivolity and cheer.

The reality was, that Christmas I stayed in my pyjamas all day, sprawled across the sofa, and watched TV. Simon cooked a proper Christmas lunch. In the second Christmas after my mother died, I was asked to go over to my cousins and uncle's house, people we always spent Christmas with when my mother was alive. But I couldn't. I felt too different to who I once was. I needed to become better acquainted with my new self before I presented myself to the world. I also didn't want to feel the pressure of having to smile or even get dressed. My father came over but wanted to leave soon after. Yet strangely, I almost enjoyed that Christmas; it asked nothing of me. I was free to be silent and stay in my pyjamas. Simon fed me. I was cocooned, cushioned and bubble-wrapped.

Those of us who do not celebrate according to the idea of the perfect Christmas are turned into species of voyeur, gazing into the homes of where Christmas is being done 'properly' via TV adverts or the boastfulness of others. It's no fun being the person who is always looking in. I had done this as child, looking into the homes of families who were functional and happy, especially at Christmas. And now, as an adult, those feelings came back to haunt me. I was back to being the girl stuck out in the cold and looking in.

'It's the grandkids and Andy on Christmas Day – and the dogs,' Donna said as she laid out old newspaper on the kitchen farmhouse table. She started to spray the pine cones gold. 'It's been like that for years now, just Andy and the kids. It's how we like it.' Donna's grandkids didn't see their mother, Donna's daughter. I found solace knowing that others also had problems with their families – I was not alone in this.

I stopped gazing out. 'I never know what I want to do at Christmas. I still don't know. I wish I could just hibernate and pop my head out when it's all over.'

'I'm here, we all are. You don't need to do anything that you don't want to do. Just do what you like,' Donna said as she let out a fizz of gold spray.

'I used to love Christmas – I was one of those annoying people shouting about Christmas in October. And now, it's one of the things I fear the most.'

'Don't hide, Kiran. I could invite my mother and siblings, but I don't want to and I'm never going to. Because, like you, I know that friends can make the best family, and family isn't always everything, no matter what people say. Families can be vile.'

'Thank you, Donna.'

'It's the truth. My friends are my family.'

It was obvious, Christmas was bound to be mercurial throughout our lives, changing with our personal circumstances: the death of a family member, a divorce, a family fallout. And as our lives changed, we would find that our Christmases no longer fitted into the old traditional mould.

'Here, help me spray the other ones, Kiran.'

I got out the silver spray, shook it vigorously and sprayed.

'Christmas feels like it's exclusive,' I said.

'How do you mean?' Donna responded.

'That it can only belong to families or children,' I said as I picked up a few more cones to spray.

'And what do you think?'

'It's the commercialism aspect, the ugly part of it, that's geared to children. The birth of Christ, goodwill to all men – hardly sounds like a notion full of childish merriment,' I replied. 'Christmas should be simple, but we've overcomplicated it. I have a friend who helps out in a homeless charity at Christmas, and another who's a nurse and she's spent many Christmases in the hospital. And some will spend it alone, with just their thoughts for company. It's not an alternative Christmas – it's their Christmas.'

'Yes – I agree!' Donna said as she handed me a fresh cup of coffee.

'I feel if we all acknowledged all the variants of the big day, and made it feel inclusive rather than exclusive, more people would be less fearful of it. We should embrace the diverse realities of Christmas! The couple who are having a happy child-free day, the pensioner who's eating Christmas lunch with the next door neighbour or the bachelor who chooses to spend the day alone with his dog. It belongs to anyone who feels the spirit of it.'

I sunk into the chair and cried. I had wanted to give this speech for so many years, but said nothing. I had never felt so much, but said so little in all those Christmases after my mother's death. But it was delivered in Donna's kitchen amongst the glitter, pine cones and metallic spray.

Christmas still belonged to me, only now it was quieter and humbler. If I chose to spend it just with Simon, it was still Christmas with the two of us and our cats. Christmas was not an altogether happy occasion, but I had come to realise that the anticipation doesn't lie in whether it's going to be a white Christmas, but in the acceptance that the day itself can contain all the four seasons.

32

SARAH, DAISY, CHARLIE AND ME

Sarah and I strolled along Llangrannog beach. It was a Sunday afternoon in December and we were walking her dogs Daisy and Charlie. I would never have thought of going to the beach in the winter, but I lived close by it. When I lived in London, I walked in Richmond Park all year round and it was beautiful. I found this to be true of the beach too.

It was a perfect day: a white winter sun with a wind that didn't suck on your face; a marbled, icy-blue sky with a foreboding streak of grey somewhere in the far-off distance, far enough not to disturb our day, but it was there and I could see it.

Daisy, a spaniel cross, was from the local rescue centre. Sarah had adopted her a few months ago and she was still new to us all. The rescue centre guessed she was 12 years old. Someone had found her tied to a street lamp in Aberystwyth. She had obviously been used for breeding and there were signs that she had been mistreated. I had gone with Sarah to see Daisy when Daisy had just been a thought. It was an unforgiving cold and wet miserable day, which added to the whole misery of the kennels. A dark, dank place of hollowness, void of any warmth and loveless. The smell was atrocious and it made its way into my hair and mouth. The clink-clank of keys, chains and locks as we walked through heavy iron gates; a prison for dogs. Everything felt so sad. I had been naive; in my head, kennels were places where dogs wagged their tails and hung around with their fellow canine friends. The man who showed us around was a strange man in his sixties, as grey and sunless as the sky. Misery grows like a fungus.

As we walked past the kennels, trying to get to the spaniel Sarah had heard of, he would sporadically stop at a kennel and tell us the background of the dog. Many of the dogs were casualties of marital break-ups. Very few times in my life had I wanted to hear a happy ending as much as I did then, listening to the man. I wished I could adopt all the dogs: a silent prayer for all those whose homes had been broken.

When we saw Daisy, she was excited to see us; humans with smiles and colour. I was wearing my Little Red Riding Hood raincoat and felt conspicuous in what was a murky sea of brown and grey. The man let Daisy out of her kennel and took her to the play area: a grey concrete square. Out of her pocket, Sarah took out a few treats and instructed Daisy to 'sit' before she was allowed to have them. She was an obedient dog, but smelt and needed a bath. Her hair was matted and in need of a trim. A few days later, Daisy was living in The Farmhouse with Sarah. Glen had arrived with dog clippers and shampoo belonging to her English Setters. And together they gave Daisy her bath.

I looked at Daisy as we all strolled along the beach, wagging her tail while she marvelled at the waves that crashed at her paws and threatened to take her out to sea. She was happy. I couldn't help but smile at her waddling along, enjoying her day; hers was a tale of happy endings.

For much of the time, Sarah and I walked in silence; we were in a happy place of crashing waves and playful dogs. We were thankful for the silence that could exist between friends who didn't feel the need to question it. The sea air allowed our thoughts to roam, languid and free. And I wondered why I ever limited the ocean, which covered more than 70 per cent of the Earth's surface, to just the summer.

I looked up and could see the old big house that I last saw when I was at the beach with Graham and Sofia in the summer.

'Sarah, that Victorian house perched at the top, I love it. It belongs in an Agatha Christie novel.' I pointed at the house that fascinated me. I loved sitting on the beach at Llangrannog and looking up at it. It stood like a beacon, its large windows keeping watch over beachgoers and the mysteries of the ocean.

'It belongs to my cousin, Christopher. It's split into two. Christopher lives at the top and the lower apartment gets rented out to holidaymakers.'

'I love that house!'

'It was built for the Archdeacon of Llandovery in 1905. That's the statue that's standing outside the house, at least I think it is. Can you see it?'

'Yes. Yes. I can see it. So many times I've looked up and wondered who it belonged to and its history. And you've known all along.' I'm not quite sure if I liked knowing the details of the house. When something is vague and unknown, the details of it are ones that you have imagined, so the thing in question belongs to you. But as soon as facts are revealed, it no longer lives within the walls of your imagination; it becomes part of the furnishings of the world.

Sarah looked at me and smiled. 'You can probably get a great view of the seals from the house.' I had never seen any seals here, but in the summer I had seen the dolphins when Graham and Sophia had visited.

During the breeding season, which was from August to December, white seal pups were often seen alone on beaches or rocky outcrops along the coast. They were fed by their mothers for three weeks, and after that they were left to fend for themselves. The mother would come to the shore every two to four hours for feeding time. She recognised her pup from its smell and call. It's thought that a pup gains up to three pounds a day from feeding on its mother's nutrient-rich milk. There had been recent disturbing news stories of seal pups dying because of humans. People had been taking selfies with pups, which disturbed their mothers nearby. The seal's mother, frightened by the commotion, would abandon her pup, leaving the pup malnourished and dehydrated. The vanity of humans had killed a few pups in this way. Everyone in the valley, including me, had been disgusted by the idea that in the quest for the perfect selfie, a vulnerable seal pup had lost its life. I reminded Sarah of the story.

'It breaks my heart,' Sarah said, 'that poor pup . . .' Sarah's heart regularly broke over stories of animals.

'Yes, poor pups. It's like we need to document ourselves standing next to great things, the great and the good and the beguiling.' I said. 'It's why we plant flags on Everest and the moon. It's the human trait of having to conquer all – to leave our mark. We stand on the highest mountains and the moon and take selfies with something the sea has conjured up. Conquering something means we possess it; a sense of ownership. They're all human trophies.'

'I think it's the ugliest part of being human,' Sarah said.

The sun hid behind the clouds and the sky was now a dove grey. I took hold of Sarah's arm. I started to feel my singularity in the world again; I began to feel like a stranger in my own life, a sense of detachment. I wasn't sure why this feeling had crept up upon me now when I could feel the closeness of a friend. I looked out to the sea and my gaze took me off to the horizon. Perhaps it was because standing next to something as old as the ocean reminded me how new everything was to me; away from London, from old friends and members of my family I still loved. I was still close to my mum's brother, my uncle, and his wife. And then their children, my cousins Jason and Selina. For a lot of my life, my immediate family and I had spent nearly all of my Christmases and Easters with this family, but I was now new in this new land. My birth, my schooldays, fond family memories, the lives of the people who touched me were far away. I was set adrift in the boundless ocean that I looked out upon, drowning in its vastness; as foreign to myself as the ocean.

The sea didn't look so friendly now that the sun had disappeared. Sarah and I walked arm in arm; I pulled her closer to me. I didn't want to drift too far out into the sea, so I held onto her like a raft: safe and anchored.

33

THE PENULTIMATE CHRISTMAS

On the walk, Sarah had told me about a sweet little church not too far away from where we lived. So the next day I decided to visit it. I sat alone in a little Welsh church in a little Welsh village. Everything was so small – the church was smaller than Wilf's shed. Anything bigger, I would have got lost in it. It was the seventh day of December and I had started to sleepwalk through the month. December had awakened the pigeon that had nested in my head when my mum died.

The church of St Bledrws, in the village of Betws Bledrws, was built in 1831. It was a charming church, gated with a little winding pathway up to it. It was the kind of church I saw in paintings. I had drifted into the church like a dream; a nomadic existence. December made me feel homeless. I wanted to spend the morning surrounded by the welcomed silence of a church. Not many people could sit with me in my silence, or even their own. I had always been vivacious. I was often told that silence didn't suit me. But silence is never silent, not when it conveys so

much. Often, when silence is present, either words aren't
adequate enough to express something, or too much has been
said and there is nothing left to be said. The years had taught me
that silence was a language only a few people were fluent in. I sat
in the pews and looked around me. Small stained-glass windows
depicted stories of Christ. I wanted to get lost in other stories,
the real Christmas story, so that my Christmas story that
rendered me motherless wasn't the only story that lived inside
my head. I needed to feel that my story ran alongside other
stories in the narration of life. My story felt less lonely that way;
it was a story amongst stories.

My mother's penultimate Christmas in 2013 was spent at my
house when I lived in London. She had been diagnosed with
womb cancer that late summer and was having chemotherapy.
She had arrived with my sister and an armful of presents. While
Simon cooked, I drove my mother and sister around Richmond
Park. It was a glorious winter day: clear, crisp and sunny. We sat
in the car and watched deer and happy people taking morning
walks before their Christmas lunch. My mother wistfully smiled
watching it all; the happiness of others entered our opened
windows. My father wasn't present. He had fallen out with me
after one of his drunken rages. We hadn't spoken for months.
So that Christmas Day lay on our chests like a heavy rock for so
many reasons.

I was broken-hearted and incredulous that Christmas.
I wanted my father. How could he not think it was important for
us to spend Christmas together as a family? How could he not

be devastated by me not being with him, like I was devastated by not being with him? Even though I dared not think it too loudly, a thought in my head wondered whether it would be our last Christmas with my mum. And I had shut down that thought, stamped it out and wrestled with it until my bones broke. Hadn't he had the same thought, even though it may have entered his head in a whisper? Sometimes quiet is loud.

I didn't give my father a Christmas present that year. It had surprised me how much the act of not giving one had hurt me. Christmas had always been so important to me, and the fact that I was unable to give my father a present broke my heart. This simple act of giving, which felt even more important in the wake of my mother's diagnosis, was made complicated. I felt that his drunken antics destroyed the precious time we had left.

My father was diagnosed with dementia, caused by alcohol, just before we went to Wales. He was admitted into a care home. His dementia wasn't that advanced. He said the odd thing now and then that reminded me he wasn't himself, but it was possible to have a lucid conversation with him. I hated that he was in a home; in his early seventies, he seemed to be the youngest person there.

When I did speak to my father, I would tell him about my day and about any big stories in the news. He told me he just stayed in his room. He didn't want to leave the four walls that now housed him and minimised his forgetfulness. And when I would visit, he would always be in his room or in the lounge with people who were clearly so much worse than he was. I know he would have hated it. The food I would bring him when I visited him in London would only be nibbled at. This person, who had always been a large figure, an erudite man who loved reading, the news and politics, was fading. His life was diminishing, closed in by clinical white walls. He was misplaced: a shark stuck in a swimming pool. He said he no longer enjoyed eating, he rarely watched TV and, even though he said he enjoyed reading, I'm not sure he was able to. His life was a self-devouring black hole getting smaller and smaller. I was afraid of the day when it would be reduced to just a pinhead. There had never been any additions of happy things in my family, just things that had been taken away: peace, childhood, life, liberty, Christmas.

I wished my parents had had a chance to get old and then die, as is the natural course of life. I wished their lives had withered and wilted in their December years. I wished my mother's life hadn't been marred by my father's alcoholism only for it to then tragically end before she was old. I wished he hadn't lost his mind over the death of his wife whom he fought with all his life due to his addiction only to then, in the sobering aftermath of her death, realise he couldn't live without her. My father unwittingly taught me that life was complicated. And even that was a gift.

I sat and remembered my dad and the Christmas of 2013 sitting in the church. It had felt easy to unravel these memories here. I had recoiled from life for so long that the surroundings of the city didn't feel safe enough for me to collapse in. I had melted into liquid and was being held together by a thin membrane. I couldn't pour myself out into the city. The city was vast; too occupied and too rapacious.

The creak of a door told me someone had come in. I slowly looked over behind me. It was a small elderly Welsh woman. We both smiled at each other. She stood in the front pew and stared at my seventh window advent calendar. She bowed her head and prayed. And then as quickly as she had come, she left. A part of me had hoped she had stayed and prompted a conversation; made a human connection.

The church smelt musty, as churches usually do. But an underlying smell of incense lingered in the air like my memories. Some things in life linger forever; you can never step out of them, nor would you want to. I had never been religious, but I was now beginning to understand my need to be out in the wilds of the countryside, to sit alone in a church and walk along the beach. All these felt eternal. Apart from the church, they were not man-made. Man-made cities and towns could no longer house me sufficiently; they malnourished me. I had been stripped to a raw state, to what felt like the very beginnings of me. I needed something that was in its raw state too, at least something that wasn't hidden, veiled or concealed in any way. I wanted to sit in the church because my experiences had humbled me. I wasn't sure the world was kind to those who used their hearts like torches, to lead them their way through life. I didn't trust the world to keep that part of me safe. I needed purity, the absence of flummery and all things that were false and untrue.

When my mother passed, I was working as a part-time GP's receptionist close to where I lived in London. A patient in his early seventies asked me if I had been on holiday, as he hadn't seen me for a while. I told him I was away because my mother had died. He looked straight at me, his eyes locked into mine. He told me his mother had died young too. And he said the most honest thing anyone had said to me up until then: that the road ahead was tough. He said there was a painting of his mother hung on his bedroom wall and that there was never a day he didn't miss her or hadn't thought about her. He said he was forever broken when his mother died and at times he still cried for her. He wished me luck on my journey and then left. Before this stranger, all I heard was '*be strong*' or '*this will pass*'. But no one spoke the truth: your pain will stay with you for the rest of your life; you will be forever altered.

The church was decorated in holly and ivy; the outdoors brought indoors. I thought about all the holly bushes around the small lanes that I lived near. Tomorrow I would take clippers and cut some of the sprigs of holly. I had a couple of cans of gold and silver spray left over from when I had upcycled furniture. I would spray sprigs of holly and decorate The Long Barn.

Two people entered the church and waved enthusiastically when I turned and looked at them. Two elderly ladies with cheeks red as holly.

'Merry Christmas!' they shouted. 'Merry Christmas,' I replied, and left.

34

THE DAY IT SNOWED

Snow had fallen from a white featureless sky. Its luminosity brightened a few days of a month that had been murky and impenetrable. And the people in the valley finally lifted their heads, no longer afraid of facing an abrasive wind that threatened to bite off their noses. The snow had been a respite from a stream of dark months.

We had only expected a few flakes of snow, but that December morning I had woken up to a bright white light, as if a spaceship had landed in the field. The huge windows of The Long Barn held the perfect scene of a snowy landscape. From every window in the house you could see it: endless snow-covered fields, separated by rows of trees. The whole valley looked like a patchwork quilt, a quilt that only cared for the colour white, the trees the crude stitching holding the patches together. I ran around the barn, wanting to look through every window, wanting to see all the angles of the valley. The windows were Christmas cards that reflected the perfect winter image, void of any interference from humans; unadulterated and immaculate. This was another window for my advent calendar.

Truffle and Blackberry looked through the windows perplexed. Blackberry would most definitely get lost in the snow – so tiny, she would drown in it.

The very steep drive that we shared with Sarah, Glen and Rod resembled a mini ski slope. With a gradient of more than 25 per cent and 70 metres in length, I couldn't imagine the car getting up it, and it would be dangerous to walk up it. Any thoughts of how we were meant to get out hadn't bothered me; I was enchanted by the new environment. But then we looked in our cupboards and fridge and freezer, and we didn't have much. We were due a grocery shop. How could we be so stupid? We were snowed in with very few supplies to keep us going. I felt annoyed at myself and Simon. We had chosen to live in the country, we should be better prepared for it. The snow had caught us out; it had come covertly under the cover of darkness. I'm sure the forecast didn't tell us there would be this much snow.

There was a knock on the door. 'Kiran, Sarah's here for you,' Simon chuckled.

Sarah stood at the doorway, perfectly dressed for the snow. She was holding two toboggans. 'I've just asked Simon if you could come out to play!'

'I'm still in my pyjamas!' I shouted from the kitchen.

'Well, put some clothes on then! Come on!'

I quickly put on my jeans and my big winter waterproof coat and a woolly hat. As soon as I walked out of the front door,

I entered a world of glorious monochrome. It was blinding. My ten-year-old self would have screamed in delight. It was perfect.

'Weeeeeeeeeeeeeeeeeeeeee!' I looked up at the sound and it was Sarah screaming her way down the steep drive in a toboggan. The sound could have caused an avalanche. Her blonde bobbed hair flew in the face of acceleration. She stopped just by our front door and without even hesitating made her way up the drive and did it all again.

I stood aghast, worried that she might hurt herself. 'Look at me!' Sarah shouted. And then off she went, speeding down our drive in a scream of giggles. Glen, Rod and Simon now stood at the bottom of the drive. And we all stared at Sarah who was on a mission to make the most of our new world. We all laughed, smiled and cheered.

'Come on, Kiran! It's bloody brilliant!' Sarah yelled as she made her way down the slope again. All of a sudden, I was gripped with fear. I had never been on a toboggan before, not even had a sleigh ride. I felt scared. Looking at Sarah, my 64-year-old neighbour, I suddenly felt old and a killjoy. I had never seen myself that way before. I had always thought of myself as someone who tried things and was open to new experiences. I had never been a stick-in-the-mud.

'Go on, Kiran!' everyone yelled.

Sarah handed me a toboggan and grabbed my hand. We trudged our way up the drive, which in the thick snow was arduous. I stood on top of the drive that I used almost every day; it was now unrecognisable.

Sarah offered her toboggan. 'Let's use one, and we can both sit on it, and I'll go down with you.'

I declined the offer: I needed to do it on my own or not at all. Rod, Glen and Simon, who were all stood at the bottom of the drive, looked up at us. 'Come on, Kiran!' Rod yelled. I looked at Sarah and she smiled and nodded. I was imagining the breakages of my bones.

The fear inside me grew branches and made its way out of my mouth: 'I'm frightened!' I said it out loud in the wide white open space, a world silenced by snowfall. I was frightened of tobogganing; of the drive that I didn't recognise any more; of the birth of yet another new world. I was frightened of letting go and frightened of holding on.

'I can't do this, Sarah.'

'Yes, you can.'

Sarah handed me a rope that was at the front of the plastic toboggan.

'Remember to stop with your feet. Now let's toboggan!!'

I tentatively listened to Sarah. What if I forgot to stop? 'I'll wait here for you and watch you go,' she said.

I had a moment to look down. Although the drop wasn't very steep, Glen, Rod and Simon looked just like three figures below. No longer people I knew, they were just few of the gazillions of people who populated the Earth. I was just a woman in the world, making her way through the life that had been given to her. I stared at the white duvet-wrapped land and then the pond that I now towered above. In the summer I had spent hours staring into that very pond. I sat in the toboggan, apprehensive; I thought I had already cracked the ice of my new world.

At high speed I whizzed down the drive and felt the world rush past me. I put out my feet and stopped just before I reached the front door. I did it, with hands shaking and heart racing. And just as I got up, Sarah, Simon, Glen and Rod pelted me with snowballs. A snowball fight ensued and all five of us threw snowballs at each other with complete abandonment.

Sarah and I became tobogganing partners that afternoon. She told me a story that years ago, when they had had the same snowfall, unable to take her car out and get to the supermarket, she had tobogganed all the way to the village. Coming out of our shared drive, if you turned left and walked up, there was a sudden sharp left and the road then cascaded all the way down to the village. And it's at that first sharp left that Sarah started to toboggan her way down. As our houses were up the foothills of the mountain, when it snowed, the roads to our homes were the last to clear. And Sarah, unable to make her way down to where the main road would be clear, decided to toboggan down to it. And from the main road, she hitched a ride to the local town and the supermarket, and then hitched a ride back home. She had whizzed down the mountain, a mile down, passing Dai's farmhouse and numerous fields, past the little beautiful bridge with the cottages and the stream and all the way down, stopping at the monument in the middle of the village. After listening to that story, I saw her as nothing short of magnificent.

With limited supplies of food, and anticipating that none of us would be able to make it to the shops, we all swapped foods that we could spare. We gave onions and carrots to the neighbours and they gave us potatoes and beans. I felt thankful of this making do of what we had. The scarcity of things made us creative and appreciative. Never in my life had I been forced to get creative because of the lack of food supplies available to me – not even as a student. And even now, it was just a minor inconvenience. In actuality, we had all that we needed – we just didn't possess all that we wanted. I was happy to be reminded of this, that no matter how bleak my life felt at times, I still lived in a world of plenty.

Before it got dark, I decided to make my way up the treacherous drive again, this time for a little walk. I turned right at the end of the drive, the turning I took for my long walks, the walk that took me to Wilf. There was no familiarity to the path any more. The world was anew – it was the world of Narnia. It was strange how snow changed the sound of things. I was used to hearing the sound of breaking twigs under my feet, the sound of birds that I couldn't identify and, of course, the sound of sheep and cattle. There would be the noise of tractors, the sound of wind, rain and hail. Even though almost always I'd walk alone on this path, some sound would accompany me. But this was a lost soundless world that I crept into. I was afraid to cough, afraid to make myself known to it. There was the soft sound of my boots on fresh snow. I heard the slight thud of snow that had fallen from a branch of a tree that had decided the snow was too heavy for it. The faint tweet of a lone bird caught my attention somewhere in the distance; a sign that something else existed other than myself. The air was thick with a silence so deafening, it became an actual sound. I was blinded by the white light of snow. It covered everything; no stream, mountain, hill or field was left uncovered. It removed the winter sleep from our eyes and awakened the child in us all. The uniformity of the new landscape took my breath away: a sea of virtuous white, unspoilt and heavenly.

I looked back from where I had come from; the only markings on the snow were my own footsteps on an untrodden and limitless world. This is what it must have felt like to be the first person to walk on the moon; the first of the adventurers; to feel the briefest contact with a world that was beyond ourselves. I was a ten-minute walk away from The Long Barn, but I could have been miles away – I *was* miles away. Within my eyeshot there were no other human dwellings. And the only sound of the tweet from the bird had vanished, the last vestige from a world that had been swallowed as I slept. This was apocalyptic Earth. The possibility of a fresh start; the first page of a journal; the chance to be the first human to walk the Earth, or at least be the only footprint in the winter snow. It was the magic of snow and the magic of new beginnings. There comes a time in our lives when all we can do is trust the world, even though we may be at war with it.

35

THE THAWING OF
SNOW AND LIFE

It took a few days before the heavy snow started to melt. Trees, bushes, rooftops, tractors and cars started to drip. Looking out towards Caer Cadwgan, the side of the valley slowly and silently melted like a scoop of ice cream. It was a slow thawing out of what had come and what had been.

Small mottled patches of earth revealed themselves as the snow disappeared on the mountain and across the valley. And just when we thought we would see a big reveal of all that had been hidden, the countryside froze again. This time, there was none of the softness of freshly fallen snow, or the gentle hypnotic drip-drip of a thawing land. The earth hardened, its nuts and bolts tightened, rendering it impervious and as friendly as a clenched fist. There was now stubborn ice as well as snow. But pockets of soft snow still existed on the mountain and on the parts of the road where the sun never shone. The conditions were now hazardous. It was unwise to walk anywhere. The glorious white had turned into a less attractive off-white.

As we had a Land Rover, our car was better suited to the conditions than our neighbours' cars, so we became the nominated drivers to do the food shop for everyone. For five days none of us had left our homes and food was running low. I had started to dream of the meals that I wanted to eat: lasagne, roast dinner, lamb curry with rice; stodgy and wholesome food. We got the shopping lists from Sarah, Rod and Glen and set off to our local town and the supermarket. I had wanted to go to see the Highlands, but it would have been foolish to drive up to the higher ground where there would have been more snow and ice. The only journeys that we could do were the ones that were essential.

As we drove down, we could see that the farmers had pushed the snow away with their tractors, creating pathways and walls of snow. The sheep across the fields looked beautiful; any photo taken would be a winning photo. The village had less snow than we had and the town only had the slush of grey snow. The ugly aftermath of something that had once been beautiful.

When we got back from the supermarket, we sensibly parked the car at the top of the drive. And then we were presented with a problem that we hadn't actually thought of: how do we get the heavy shopping bags down the veritable ski slope that was our drive? I was already feeling apprehensive of walking down the slippery, snowy, icy drive. But to do it while carrying heavy shopping, I was certain the weight of the bags would propel me forward, causing me to unwillingly ski down. Thankfully, we noticed that the toboggans had been left on the side of the top of the drive. So we put the shopping bags in the toboggans and then let the groceries whizz down the slope. They lost their high-speed momentum as they got closer to our front door and came to a gentle halt. Amazingly, the novel transport only lost a packet of Jaffa Cakes and a bag of pasta en route. With great caution, we slowly managed to walk down the drive without slipping and sliding. I felt a sigh of relief when we reached our front door.

That evening we had a dinner of chicken pie with mashed potatoes. It was what I had dreamed of: food that felt like a hug. And after dinner I toasted marshmallows on the fire; sticky and gooey. I sat in my pyjamas and stared into the flames and thought about the last few days: the snow that kept us hostage, the tobogganing and the thawing and then the freezing of the valley. And I had one of those moments again, a feeling of being a stranger in my own life. I couldn't be living a more contrasting life to the one that I had always known. I sat crossed-legged, watched the flames dance and realised I had never taken time to stop and stare, not really. I had stared at the bigger things, not the little things; not at the nuances of life. I had been a human pinball machine, catapulted from one distraction to the next.

Occasionally, I would throw a bit of wood into the fire, poke it around a bit and then watch it burn. At first the log would flare up, then blacken and fall into pieces, eventually meeting its fate: becoming embers of a dying fire. Everything burned brightly and then just flickered in life.

A few years ago, on this very day in the December of my mother's life, I sat with her in a hospital room that was stuffy and airless. The place where she would spend the last six weeks of her life. She sat up in the armchair while I sat in a chair opposite her. It was rare for me to be alone with her; her siblings, my gran, my sister, family friends and my father were a constant presence. Christmas carols from a radio somewhere flooded the room. In the past few months her existence had got smaller and smaller; she occupied less space. She could hardly walk now, though she insisted that we walk her up and down the hospital ward as she held onto one of us. She had stopped watching the TV; it was almost always switched off. The light of a TV screen should never outshine your own, and her light was fading. That morning, on the radio, the astronomer Martin Rees said: 'The chemical elements in our universe are made from star explosions – we are the ashes of dead stars.' My mother was like a star that I held in the eyepiece of a telescope that was getting harder and harder to locate.

A few days before, my sister and I (we were still speaking to each other at that point) had had a meeting with two doctors and a Macmillan nurse. Mum had just been admitted a few days before December with problems with her kidney. My sister and I sat in the meeting hopeful. I was in a sunken armchair full of superfluous fabric. I could see that the doctors were moving uncomfortably in their chairs.

'Would you like your mother to go home now?' one of the doctors asked.

I was confused. 'No, she's fine here. She's being taken care of, why move her?'

And then the Macmillan nurse said what the doctors had been avoiding: 'Where do you want your mother to die?' The armchair I was sitting on swallowed me. The cup of tea that I was holding dropped to the floor; a sign of diminished civility.

Back in the airless room my mother sat, small, fragile and hairless. Even though it was just the two of us, silence became a guest that sat between us; a reckoning of this new reality of our lives. And then she broke the silence.

'I want you to do something. I want you to thank God that you have a good husband. He looks after you. He's not like your dad. I don't need to worry about you.'

Tears that I didn't feel coming streamed down my face. I nodded, agreeing that I had married someone who was kind and thoughtful; who handled me with care. All of life came down to this: the treatment of others and the love that we express. And my mum and I both unravelled this truth of life in this strange white box of a room; the waiting room for the afterlife; the last room that we would both be alive in.

I panicked as streams of my life flashed before me: my strong-willed nature as a child and my rebellious teenage years.

'Mum.'

'Yes?'

'I'm sorry! If I ever broke your heart, I'm sorry. Please forgive me,' I pleaded.

My mother sat still, strangely still. She replied without the urgency that my own words carried.

'Children do break their parents' hearts. It's the way of the world. When you're young, you have a fire that burns inside you, and that's the way it should be. But you've never disappointed me. You have always been so kind, helpful and intelligent.'

'Mum, the rest of them, they're not like us. We have the same heart.' My siblings and father were always so complicated, self-destructive. In my mother, I had an ally. Please don't leave me alone with them, I thought.

'I know you've all done all that you could to save me.'

I broke while my mother spoke with unwavering equanimity and grace. I was so relieved that she had her faith; it was her faith that was seeing her through the dark tunnel she looked down.

My mother seemed unmoved by my tears. It was as though she had reached some other realm; a place of otherness. She stared at something that I couldn't see. Even though she sat opposite me, she was far away.

My mother's life, the beginning and now her end, opened up in front of me like a book. And I couldn't bear to look at it. It was full of woe and complications. I didn't see her life like that pre-cancer, but you can only judge a life when it comes to an end, because only then can you see the whole story. We had all suffered so much. I needed to hear something good, something to help assuage this burden of a life thwart with difficulties.

'Mum, tell me your life hasn't been all bad? Tell me you felt some love, some joy in it! We did have some good times, didn't we? Remember how much fun we had in France? And we went to Portugal and Spain and . . .'

I was like some crazed woman, desperate for evidence of sunnier days. I couldn't bear to think my mother would die without really living.

'There are many women who have tough lives, but I am lucky. I had some good times. And I found Jesus.'

I believe my mum knew what I needed to hear: she knew what it was to feel happy and she would not be alone.

We were no longer having a casual mother and daughter talk, like we used to. We were having a conversation, human to human. Two people whose worlds had been reduced to this one room. We had both been stripped to the very nucleus of who we were.

36

MY BIRTHDAY

The 20th day of December was my birthday. My eyes opened in
a wide panic as I lay in bed. It wasn't the panic of something as
shallow as getting older; it was the panic of being thrown into
yet another pool of a memory that I thought would kill me. But
no matter how painful a memory is, it's a remnant of something
that has survived. A painful memory is a token of your survival,
not of your demise.

It was on my 40th birthday in 2014 that the hospital asked me
to say goodbye to my mother. I whispered in my mother's ear that
it was OK for her to leave us. The syringe driver, a constant
round-the-clock pain relief used at the end of life, had been put
in her leg and she was no longer conscious, even though we were
told she would still be able to hear us. On the anniversary of the
day my mother had been in hospital giving birth to me, she was
now in hospital leaving me. On this day, 40 years ago, we had
shared a bed, day one of our life together. Now, I thought, it's our
last day together. My uncle had prayed that my mother would

hang on, just for another day, and not die on my 40th. Alone in the room with my mother, I took my index finger and drew a cross on her forehead. I then followed a throbbing, pulsating green vein on the side of her head; it made its way through my finger and up my arm and synchronised with the beat of my heart. I wished life had been kinder to her. I knelt beside her bed, put my head down and placed her fragile papier-mâché hand on my head and sobbed into the bedsheets: my 40th birthday.

In the hot, airless hospital room, we were all a constant presence on that 20th day of December, as we had all been since she had been admitted in the last few days of November. The seconds between each laboured breath of my mother grew longer. December: the month we had watched her body decay. The cancer that had entered her like a thief in the night had resided in her body like a squatter. It was as if an eraser was slowly rubbing out her existence, day by day. And we were all forced to watch. My gran, her mother, had cursed God for letting her life drag out for us all to witness: 'Even God doesn't take her!' Just before she went into a coma, I had watched her sleep. And every time she woke up, her eyes would open suddenly and dart around the room, as if she was surprised that she was still here.

That afternoon, my mother was still with us, alive, not as expected. I left my mother's hospital room and went for a walk around the ward. Everyone else stayed in the room. I needed to get out. I needed to breathe. We had all been visiting the room for 22 days – 22 days of watching someone you love slip away. But it wasn't so much of a slipping away; it was far more brutal than that. She had been in unbearable pain. Her kidneys failed, she was gasping for breath, she was desperate for water that we had to refuse her because she could no longer swallow. And every day, the air in the room got heavier and heavier. I knew what it was: it was death making itself at home. It had slipped underneath the door, when no one had been looking, and lurked in the corner. For weeks it swam around the room, teasing us by creating shadows on the walls – we had all tried to ignore it. We prayed it would leave, but like a leech sucking on blood, it had sucked the oxygen out of the room. We had all hoped that my mother would miraculously pull through, even though we had diagrams, reports and images that told us otherwise. Hope is often kept like a secret, in between words that have been spoken and words that we dare not speak. We fear that in the wrong hands or seen with the wrong eyes our hope will be ridiculed, or worse, broken.

Walking around the ward I could not help but notice all the Christmas trees and tinsel – they felt intrusive and callous. A carol flooded out of someone's room:

> Hark! The herald angels sing,
> 'Glory to the newborn King!
> Peace on earth and mercy mild,
> God and sinners reconciled.'
> Joyful, all ye nations rise,
> Join the triumph of the skies,

The carol set off some sort of whirlpool in my brain. I could feel the actual flooding of my mind; an intensity of feeling and emotion; a dam bursting. It forced me to swim to the very deepest parts of me. I tried to walk out of the building and opened the door of the ward into the corridor. But I crumpled; my legs were about to give way. Just as I opened the door, a lady, probably in her early fifties, walked through. She was carrying a tower of Christmas presents. 'What's the matter, love?' She had a soft Irish accent. I felt the flooding again and a desperate need to pour myself out into the world. 'My mum, she's dying. She's dying from cancer!' The lady ushered me out of the corridor and put her presents down on the floor. She hugged me tight. 'I know your journey – my father had cancer. I know the ups and downs of it all, the good news and then the bad news.' She then touched the side of my face. 'What's your mother's name, my love?' My vision was blurred with all the flooding. 'Her name is Piari. My mother's name is Piari.' The lady repeated my mother's name. 'I'm going to church this evening. I will say a pray for you and your dear mother.' And then she hugged me again, stranger to stranger.

On my birthday in my first year in Wales, I lay in bed as Simon got my birthday breakfast ready. I heard the sounds of cupboard doors opening and closing; the kettle boiling; the opening of the oven door. I had never been a person who enjoyed a lie-in. If I stayed in bed, it was because I couldn't face the day, not because I enjoyed sleep. I had stopped sleeping years ago when my mother was diagnosed with cancer. It led to an addiction to sleeping pills. Sleep, when it came, was a respite from my pain in those final days of my mother's life. How could one sleep when the tick-tock of time was felt so profoundly? It was strange living with this impenetrable sleeplessness. I had often felt there was nothing to do in life since she died. I hadn't wanted to live, so I may as well have slept my life away. When she did die, I understood pain in a way I had never understood before. I understood in that moment the depths people will go to to have that pain taken away, the kind of place you would need to be in emotionally to self-harm. Although I never did it myself, I had imagined it many times. I imagined slitting my skin and allowing all that pain my body was too small to house dripping out of me in an exquisite relief. I just didn't know what to do with so much pain. And yet, I felt the urgency of life; the frailty of it; the beauty, the depth, the mystery and the pain of it. How could I sleep when I knew and felt so much?

A table full of presents, croissants and fresh coffee stood ready for me on the kitchen table. I sat in my pyjamas and opened cards and presents. In between opening each new card, I would pause to look out of the kitchen window: the advent calendar window for the 20th day of December. The windows were big enough to let all of nature look in as well as for us to look out; a mutual admiration of all our positions in nature. The valley centred me, not because we rotated around it as we got on with the daily mundane duties of our lives but because I always knew where I was when I looked at it. It was like a compass: if I looked at it, I knew where I was. When I lost focus, it held me in its gaze. Since the summer party, I regarded it as important as the Parthenon in Athens.

When I was child in middle school, from the ages of nine to twelve, the school tradition was to bring in sweets on the day of your birthday. And every year, the day before my birthday, my father would take me to the shops and we would buy the biggest tin of Roses or Quality Street we could find. I longed to be that girl again, but just in that snapshot of a memory, with nothing either side of it, no past and no future. Just a girl holding her father's hand on her way to buy sweets with a smile as wide and colourful as a rainbow.

When I was younger, I always thought that any gaps in our lives eventually got filled with other things. Voids were temporary states, like a missing filling in a tooth that you can't stop feeling with your tongue. Then you visit the dentist who fills it, and your tongue runs over it again and it feels like there had never been a hole. And the history of the hole in your tooth just disappears – you forget there ever was one. But this wasn't true of life. The deepest voids in our lives are never filled. It is something we like to believe, a nice story that we tell ourselves, that we can bounce back and feel whole again. I felt liberated by understanding this wasn't true. Perhaps I wasn't meant to go through life feeling whole. Perhaps in acknowledging and feeling the void I allowed myself to feel my whole self? Accepting this stopped me from shoving a load of rubbish into the cavities of my life; square pegs into round holes. The holes in my life were permanent, and the trick was not to fall into them.

Sat at my breakfast birthday table, I had become acutely aware of how different I was to how I used to be. I often wondered how friends and family would take this new version of me. Did I let them down by not being as enthusiastic about things like my birthday or the ease with which I let things pass? And that was what was the most appealing part of starting a new life: no one knew the person that I had once been. They didn't know my birthday would have been spent drinking cocktails and eating in a posh London restaurant. I was just someone unassuming, curious about the Welsh countryside and the lives of the people I met. I enjoyed my slow birthday morning, mostly because I was given the space and time to uncoil into the day. I think that's one of the most loving things anyone could have done for me: acknowledge that I had changed and let me slowly breathe into my new existence. We are never the people we once were. We have many, many metamorphoses.

Glen had come in as I sat in my pyjamas in the kitchen drinking coffee, surrounded by a mountain of wrapping paper and cards. 'Happy Birthday!' She dropped off a present – a woolly hat to go with my Little Red Riding Hood raincoat. Soon after, just before leaving for work, Sarah dropped off a card and a present – a lantern. *'Happy Birthday to my lovely friend!'*

In the evening, we had driven up to Caer Cadwgan for a birthday drink. When I opened the unusually dark kitchen, the kids and Donna and Andy sprung out. 'Happy Birthday!' Birthday banners and poppers exploded in the air like mini fireworks. And we all fell over in a bundle of laughter: innocent, beautiful, uncomplicated. And Donna was hosting a surprise birthday dinner for me with the kids, Andy and Simon.

'*Happy Birthday to you, Happy Birthday to you, Happy Birthday dear Kiran . . . Happy Birthday to you!*'

'Oh, this is just lovely! Thank you everyone.'

'Go on, Andy, get the birthday girl a glass of bubbly,' Donna shouted.

The kids wished me birthday greetings, handed me homemade cards, gave me a kiss and a hug and then ran into the living room to watch TV. Simon, Andy, Donna and I toasted the day.

Donna had laid out the dinner table with so much thought and attention to detail. A cream tablecloth; dark green placemats; crisp white napkins secured with a gold stag clip. I took a moment to take it all in: the country kitchen, a dark starry night; Rosie the horse in her stable just a stone's throw away, all the other animals in the smallholding and Donna, Andy and all the kids; my homemade cards. It was all so wholesome.

'Your birthday menu, Kiran. Starter: garlic mushrooms. For the main: sirloin steak with onion rings, grilled tomatoes and homemade chips. And for dessert, I've made you a chocolate cake.'

'All that is just bloody perfect. Thank you.'

'Now, you don't need to keep thanking me. You're family.'

I looked around my surprise birthday dinner table. Apart from Simon, not that long ago these people had been unknown to me. They would have been strangers who I walked passed in a supermarket. And now we sat around a dinner table sharing food cooked in the honour of my birthday. Society and my Indian culture made so much of the idea of blood, and yet I cared so very little for it. 'Family is everything': a mantra designed to keep toxic relationships alive. Freedom came from knowing that the people I was tied to via blood were not the people I had to stick with. I was free to roam and find a milieu of my own creation. I no longer had to sacrifice my emotional well-being for the sake of toxic family members. I was a seed in the eye of a storm across the ocean that landed on an island and fruited. A brown paper bag blowing down the street on an autumnal day. A bird with a damaged wing that still soared foreign heights. This was the great unbecoming of me.

37

CHRISTMAS EVE

As Simon prepared food on Christmas Eve, ready for the next day, I felt the wanderer in me, so I put on my walking boots and made my way to the great outdoors. As soon as I got out of the steep drive and turned right, I knew it was where I needed to be. The landscape welcomed me with open arms. I could breathe.

What I loved most about being in the countryside was that I could escape into the Welsh hills; I always felt like I was walking into a painting.

Branches quaked timidly in the wind. The air was imbued with the pleasant, dewy petrichor of rain that had fallen overnight. Brave birds flew higher and faster in a wind that wouldn't give up. My only company was the beat of my own raging heart. It felt as though it existed outside my body, a separate entity. Out in the wilds, I had become so well acquainted with it, my heart. *Hello, Heart.* My heart walked alongside me on this solitary walk on Christmas Eve, the anniversary of my mother's death.

A day, a few hours, a few minutes had changed the course of my life. Since that day, I was scared of the 24th day of December; scared to exist in that one day. As soon as a new year started, I could feel the 24th day of December heading towards me. None of the other days really mattered; they were just stepping stones to this one day. How odd to feel the insignificance of the 364 other days; to make life just about one day and then be afraid to live in that one day.

I passed Wilf's shed. I could see that his light was on: 'Every day is the same for a farmer, even at Christmas.' For the first time, I didn't pop in to say hello to Wilf. Some walks in life must be done alone; undisturbed, like a ghost wandering the Earth. My curiosity didn't lead me to Wilf's shed as it usually did, wanting to ask him questions, wondering about a life that was so different to mine. Today, my curiosity widened to the bigger mysteries of the world. So I carried on walking and passed Wilf's shed without stopping. I walked up the small incline towards the Roman road and stopped and turned around to look at Wilf's shed. Things looked different at a distance. The shed, a farmer, this land: in all this, I was a visitor.

I could feel the footprints of every person who had once walked this land, behind me and in front of me. They walked with me in solidarity. They had walked the same arduous journey and were wiser for it. They had survived. One foot in front of the other: keep walking. Life exists because of one move: one foot in front of the other. My feet fitted into the moulds of previous walkers; their feet had been cast in the earth. I had never felt so comfortable fitting into a mould. Where there are footprints, there had once been life.

I had never realised that the simple act of walking was such a powerful tool: you can walk away. Socrates was a well-known walker, one of life's meanderers. The fresh air made me feel alive. I was alive. Alive. Alive. *Alive.* Even though I had thought this day would have killed me. Some experiences maim us. We may not have lost a leg or an arm, but something that was part of us has gone. And after the maiming, we are different. Forever changed.

I took my time to look at the undulating land cloaked in the barrenness of winter; a world shutting down. I remembered when the nurses took the drip away from my mother's bedside. My father, who slept on the floor on a mattress beside my mother's bed for 26 days, was the first to say something. We were all in the room. 'The drip's gone,' my father said. And Simon, who stood by the window that he had slightly opened to let some air in, said they had taken it away that afternoon. And my father said something that I can still hear, after all these years. He said, 'Why have they taken it away … how is she going to live?' I remember that very moment, how innocent his question was, how much we were all in denial, and how the question hung in the room for us all to wrestle with. I remember it was just about to get dark and the sky was beautifully marbled with a pink hue. In the distance we could hear church bells ringing. The removal of the drip was like the dismantling of a pop-up theatre: the show was over; there was nothing left to see; the props were being carted away. '*All the world's a stage, And all the men and women merely players.*'

I carried on walking and took in the countryside and stared at the bare trees and fields, once green and lush. I had always imagined what it must be like to be in the wilds of Africa. I imagined that such places made you totally forget yourself because you would be so immersed in the landscape and wildlife. Places that made you forget all other worlds. The landscape here was like the wilds of Africa for Wilf. A place where he became totally absorbed in the landscape; a place where he forgot himself. What a rare and wonderful thing that must be: to totally forget. Standing now, looking all around me, I could almost see how Wilf saw the world. I was a finite being held in the palm of a spinning rock that we called Earth.

I could hear myself talking to the trees, the bushes, the insects, the rabbits and the birds. Even though I couldn't see any rabbits or insects, I didn't feel like I was speaking out into a void; I was talking to nature and I was a part of it. I had an inexplicable desire to tell nature my story; to unravel myself in the midst of it, like the leaves that had fallen and the earth that had eroded.

I didn't feel lonely walking around in this vast space on my own, not now. Even in the muffled winter silence of it. I was part of a bigger picture, part of this interconnected natural world. I had become so familiar with the landscape and the trees that I realised something. Through all those solitary walks I had taken throughout the seasons, I had never walked alone; nature had walked with me.

I still wondered if my mother had chosen to pass when no one was there, in the early hours of Christmas Eve while we all slept.

And then we had that dreaded call and we arrived at the hospital between 2 and 3am. Her laboured breathing had stopped. Her chest that pumped up and down begging to stay alive so fiercely now lay dormant. In death, her face looked shocked, her mouth open, as if death had taken her by surprise. The light from the little lamp by the hospital bed seemed less harsh. There was a soft pink glow about the room. And for a moment, the deafening silence of it all crept into my chest and stopped my heart. Her body, an empty vessel of nothingness. Then and there, I understood what was meant by someone's 'spirit'.

All of us, my father, sister and my mother's family, stood in this thick silence. I asked Simon to open the window; I needed the heaviness to leave the room. I think I heard the sound of distant church bells ringing, welcoming Christmas, and I wondered, upon hearing them, if my mother's spirit had slipped out of the window and into the early morning.

The night before, my mother's sister-in-law, my favourite aunt, told my mother to leave, that she could let go. She had clung onto life for weeks. Even the doctors said they were amazed at how long she lasted. It had been torture for us; she fought for life, even when there was no hope for it. My aunt begged her to stop fighting now; there was nothing left in this world for her except pain. She told my mother we could no longer watch this slow, dragged-out, inevitable death. Jesus was waiting for her, and she must go; it was the only place she could be free now. A few hours later, my mother left this world.

It was still dark when we left the ward in the early hours of

Christmas Eve. We all dispersed and the talk of funeral arrangements started. It had just gone 5am. Simon and I drove home in silence. Classic FM was on quietly in the background and the instrumental version of 'Walking in the Air' was playing. I looked at my hands – they appeared and felt different; so empty, they felt heavy.

Years later, I know what that feeling was. It was that real primal fear you have when you are a child and you're shopping with your mother and for a moment your mother's hand slips. And for a brief few seconds panic sets in, you can no longer feel your mother, she has left your hand empty. And then you see your mother and hold hands again, and all's well in the world. I realised, from now on, my hand would always be empty. I looked out of the window as we passed a 24-hour petrol station, street lamps, a fox and rows of houses. They all looked different to me now: alien. The world had altered: a removal of order, boundaries and civility. I felt a detachment from all the earthly things that had once made sense to me: books, time, maps, hospitals, roads. There was a strange mix in that early Christmas Eve morning. It was that feeling of magic that one gets in the early hours of Christmas Eve and Christmas Day. These two days never feel ordinary. It's a feeling that I had carried with me all my life, since I was a kid, like we all do. This feeling was now mixed with a crushing emptiness. An emptiness that felt like an unrelenting pressure that would break me. All I could feel was the weight of a void. And the rhythms of the earth that vibrated under my feet just reverberated the banality of life.

I was afraid of the raw openness that I had started to feel. Anything could hurt me. I was frightened by the enormity of the feelings that swirled around inside me. But a life half-felt is a life half-lived. Sometimes just living is an act of bravery. There is a misconception about the umbilical cord. It is never cut at birth, but severed in death.

The wind picked up again and my nose started to drip. I thought about Simon in the kitchen preparing food for Christmas lunch. I had always wanted Christmas as a kid, but it was always ruined by my father's alcoholism, and then in the later years we had the Christmases that I wanted. Now, with my mother's death on Christmas Eve, I understood Christmas was never meant for me. I was transported back to being the little girl who always looked into the happy homes of others. I didn't feel anger towards my father for the bad memories caused by him. I just hung onto all the good things about him. There was now a far bigger feeling than the feeling of anger, and that was the feeling of deep impenetrable sadness. And the lasting residual feeling I had was love.

Watching my father cry uncontrollably over my mother's dead body on Christmas Eve, I felt the futility of it all. It was too late to be sorry now. Too late to declare his love for her. Too late to tell her she had always been right. And too late to admit he had been a fool. As I stood by watching my father break, I felt the wastefulness of life. And it made me shudder.

I reached The Long Barn. It all looked, smelt and felt so

homely. 'Did you have a nice walk, darling?' Simon said as he gave me a tight hug.

'Yes, thanks.'

'Sarah popped in – she dropped off some flowers for you and your mum.'

I touched the lilies that Simon had placed in a vase: a token of love, thought and care.

'How nice of her to remember.' Thank God for friends.

38

A VERY ORDINARY CHRISTMAS

Sadness comes to us in moments of quiet; in whiffs of melancholy creeping in through the back door of our lives. It's the same for joy too. On Christmas Day morning I felt an unexpected joy: a quiet joy. I woke up to a misty valley. The sheep on the side of the valley looked serene. Christmas carols played gently in the background; Classic FM was on the radio in the kitchen. There was a stillness to the morning.

The Christmas tree lights were on and Simon was already in the kitchen getting the day ready. Rod, Glen and Sarah had been invited over for Christmas lunch. And in the evening, Simon and I would be seeing Donna and Andy and the kids. I crossed my legs and sat on the sofa by the Christmas tree and looked out at the valley and allowed myself to absorb the morning. It was still a little dark and I could see the lights on at the white farmhouse where Tess and Andrew lived. There was still one thing that I loved about Christmas: you could guess what most households were doing. I guessed that both Tess and Donna would be in the kitchen. But this year I thought about the farmers I knew too, Dai and Wilf. And I could guess, rather accurately, what they would be doing: the same as they were doing yesterday and the day before that.

The morning was spent opening presents by the tree. Presents from my London family, in-laws and the neighbours. Truffle and Blackberry played with catnip-filled toys Sarah had bought them and then dived into the wrapping paper and played with ribbons. The Christmas church service was on TV, as it had always been on our Christmas Day mornings. We ate a breakfast of crumpets with butter and maple syrup with a pot of fresh coffee, just as we always did on Christmas morning. When I was a kid, we would all go to church for the 10am service. I called my father at the home. He said he didn't know it was Christmas, and that made me cry.

I got dressed and started to help out in the kitchen. The potatoes for lunch had come from our garden. The turkey had come from Donna and Andy's smallholding. Glen would be bringing pavlova for dessert. I realised that Christmas Day had its own mechanics. I had never really thought about it before, because I had never had to rely on it for my survival before. The routine of opening presents in the morning; the time to put the turkey in the oven; the precise time to put the vegetables on; the time the church service comes on TV; the time when the guests arrive; the time when *The Snowman* comes on TV; the time to get the Christmas cake out. This whole structure of Christmas Day is like some giant scaffolding decorated with tinsel. And

I realised that if I used this framework and observed the regimented timings of the day, it could save me. There was little room to deviate from the order: I was a happy slave to the mechanics of the day. Every year for the past seven years, after my mother died, when I had thrown out the order of the day and just went with the flow of how I felt, I drifted. I drifted to the very darkest parts of me. And now I was ushered along the hours of the day with a sense of doing; it lifted me from any dark hole that I had the potential to fall into.

It's strange how many of the things that we come to fear are in fact very ordinary; no monsters or ghouls chasing us, just days that come to mean something to us. In the end, we fear the ordinary. Death is ordinary; death is so everyday. I feared tinsel and Christmas crackers and all that was synonymous with the season. It is the ordinary that gets us in the end.

I laid out the table and decorated it in gold and silver holly, tasted the gravy, gave it the thumbs up and opened a bottle of Prosecco.

When we had returned to the hospital at 10am the day my mother died to collect her belongings, I had asked a man in scrubs where the office was in the hospital that I needed to collect her things from. I burst out crying when I asked him the question and then blurted out that my mother had died at 62 from cancer in the early hours of that morning. The man in scrubs escorted Simon and me to the office, which was just around the corner by the hospital's coffee shop that had a noticeably long queue. Some minutes later, while I we sat in the office, there was a knock on the office door. It was the man in scrubs. He didn't say anything, just handed Simon and me a hot chocolate each that he had queued for in the cafe. And as he handed me the large cup, he held my hand, ever so briefly. If it had been a word, it would have been a whisper. But it was there, a communication of feeling: stranger to stranger, human to human.

As I stood amongst the peelings of potatoes, drinking Prosecco, listening to the slight murmur of the oven, amongst the paraphernalia of the day, I remembered that kind man in scrubs. He was dark-haired, probably in his late thirties. But I remembered him, away from London, out in the quietude of the Welsh countryside, after all these years. And the Irish lady who said she would pray for my mother. And all the people in the cafe who had witnessed me drunk on grief, the lady who had lost her daughter to cancer, the priest who blessed me in the cafe, the waiter who told me my mother was in a better place. I remembered them all, like I always did at this time of year. They were now my Christmas story. Just as people bring out the nativity set at Christmas, these nameless people, who touched my life with such brevity, were brought to the forefront of my mind. Along with my mother, they were forever in my thoughts, stitched into the very fabric of my being. I prayed for them and wished them a Happy Christmas – just as I did for my mother every Christmas Day. Unaware to them, they were now part of my life, forever.

Glen and Rod were the first to arrive. And then Sarah

arrived soon after. We were all out of our 'country clothes'. I had that kind of feeling you get when you're a kid and you are playing 'grown-ups'. This is how I felt sans our usual country attire. We shared food, stories and our lives.

That evening, when we had come back from Donna and Andy's, I stood on the balcony and looked out into the darkness. I saw that the lights were still on at Donna and Andy's. It had gone past 1am. I held a cup of tea in my hand and looked inside the warm glow of our living room. The fire was on and the cats were stretched out in front of it. I was the little girl looking in, but this time I was looking into my own home, not other people's. And I liked what I saw and heard: an absence of drama, anger and complication.

Christmas Day went by placidly, joyfully and uneventfully. Just five grown-ups enjoying each other's company. The lack of drama made me realise how much anxiety Christmas evoked in me. From being a child and wanting to have Christmas like any other family who didn't have an alcoholic for a father, it had meant so much to me. And then in recent years, being a grown-up and trying to make Christmas perfect, because I had lost so many Christmases in my childhood. And all that Christmas anxiety reached a crescendo in 2014 when my mother died. All that accumulation of anxiety had crippled me. I had vowed to never care about Christmas again. Soon it would be spring.

39

THE NEW YEAR'S EVE SWIM, DAFFY, TESS AND ME

Tess had convinced me to go for a New Year's Eve swim at New Quay beach. Having never entered the sea in the UK before – I only went in on holiday abroad when the temperature was scorching – and just once taking my shoes off and walking along the seashore, the idea of going for a winter swim in Wales filled me with dread. I was a foreigner to these shores.

I had agreed to go for a winter swim because things were different now. I was different; everything was anew. Where there once would have been a 'no', there was now a 'yes'. Over the years, grief had weakened me. I had become a weak link. The gravity that pulled me to the Earth became more of a limp handshake than a forceful hand that secured my feet on the ground. I realised that acknowledging this made room for a new dawn. So I had become less fearful of my rootless world. Rootless meant I was a wanderer in life; it was nothing to be afraid of, it was what I had always been. I felt the limits and constraints of space and time. Time waits for no one – it's committed to the future. I wanted to see, touch, feel as much beauty as I could in this world. Prisms of raindrops; a human connection; the early morning mist; a dancing butterfly; the rise of the sun: the catalyst to numerous possibilities. Inside me lived a curiosity for life that gnawed away at me from the inside out. And it told me that, even though my world had darkened, there was still some light. If I couldn't be and do more after the experiences of the last several years, I wasn't sure what all those experiences had been for. To do more and be more was a way of honouring those experiences; it was me grabbing life's face with both hands and whispering: I heard you. The obvious and natural by-product of any adventure or a deeply felt experience is for us to change. And usually we are better people for it, our awareness elevated. So I said 'yes' to Tess.

She often swam with a group called The Blue Tits, a group of women of all ages who got together for a swim in various swimming spots, whatever the weather. The Blue Tits would be swimming on New Year's Eve and we would be joining them.

New Year's Eve was a cold, sunny and clear day. It was on New Year's Eve that we buried my mother, seven days after she died. I had written a eulogy. I talked about her strength and grace, and how she laughed her way through life – even in the face of adversity. My mother was known for her big smile and her laughter. Only the brave smile in the dark.

Tess beeped. I looked out of the window and I could see her frantically waving from her red jeep. Everything with her was exciting, wonderful and new. She was part of a rowing group and once rowed from Wales to Ireland. I couldn't believe that I was about to get into the sea on such a cold and frosty morning. But what else would I do on the day that I buried my mother? Like Christmas Eve, New Year's Eve was another one of those days that was imbued with so much and yet felt the emptiest of days. I walked aimlessly around the hours of those days desolate but full of pain. I never knew life could be so paradoxical.

Tess and Andrew kept geese and chickens and had two Border Collies called Teddy and Mac. In the car on our drive to the beach, Tess started to tell me a curious story about a duck called Daffy.

Tess had noticed that one of the duck eggs for hatching was not being sat on by the mother duck. Duck eggs need a higher hydration to hatch, so worried that the duckling might be weak and need help hatching, she kept the neglected egg on her bedside table and kept it warm and hydrated by using a damp cloth. One night the egg started to hatch. Tess gently helped the duckling, but tried not to intervene more than was necessary. And there, in Tess and Andrew's bedroom, Daffy was born. He soon became part of their family. The duck would sit on the sofa with Andrew and Tess when they watched TV. When they took the dogs for a walk, Daffy went too. The dogs and Daffy had adventures together; they crossed and swam streams together and took long walks in the valley. Daffy would eat with the dogs – they didn't mind sharing their bowls with the duck; they accepted him. When Tess and Andrew went to bed, Daffy would sit at the bottom of the stairs and get all hysterical and cry until Tess brought him up the stairs to be with them. In the evenings, Daffy would want cuddles on the sofa and Tess would put a blanket under him and he would snuggle in between Tess and Andrew. Daffy had a daily routine of picking and cleaning the dogs' ears, which the dogs didn't seem to mind – it had become a part of their playtime with Daffy. Daffy had decided that Tess, Andrew and Mac and Teddy were his family, and he loved them just as much as they loved him. After a few months, Tess tried to integrate him with the rest of the geese, ducks and chickens. At first he had cried when he was put in the pen, and frantically quacked until Tess took him out again. And then slowly, over the weeks, he had got used to his new family, and they welcomed him. Gradually, he started to spend more time with his new family than his old. But whenever he wanted a cuddle or a bit of fuss made over him, he would pop in to see his old family and resume some of his former habits. One day, Tess noticed that Daffy wasn't quite himself; he was lethargic. And then something happened that broke Tess's heart: Clyde, the gander, got Daffy by the neck and killed him. Clyde had never shown any aggression before, so it puzzled both Andrew and Tess why he had suddenly turned on the duck. Tess told me her theory of why Daffy was killed. She believed that Clyde knew Daffy was sick, and it made the flock vulnerable, so he killed him.

As silly as it may seem, when Tess had finished telling me the story, I felt tearful. For Tess, it was one of many wonderful stories she had, but for me, it was a remarkable story of two worlds that I would have thought would never mix. I had never seen ducks as sentient creatures; dogs and cats, yes, but a duck that made a home within four walls and cried when he felt lonely injected me with a sense of wonder.

'I was devastated when Clyde killed him. He was such lovely boy, you would've loved him, Kiran.'

This was a story of displacement. 'It reminds me of the cuckoo,' I commented.

'The cuckoo?'

'The cuckoo lays its eggs in other birds' nests.'

'Yes, it does.'

'Daffy's egg hatched in your bedroom – a kind of displacement. As is the cuckoo's egg in the reed warbler's nest. Both eggs were put in places you'd think they really shouldn't be in. And yet Daffy and the cuckoo's young flourished. You'd think the cuckoo wouldn't survive with birds not of its kind, and that Daffy could never make a home with dogs and humans. And yet, they did – and thrived.'

'Yes, Daffy considered us his family.'

'Daffy's story and the cuckoo's story are about homes – unlikely homes, homes that shouldn't really work but somehow do.'

'Yes, life is strange, isn't it?'

'Yes, it is rather.'

The gloriously cold and sunny day brought many people to the beach. I was surprised at how busy it was. Tess and I walked and laughed our way to the beach, holding our bags that contained a change of clothing: big thick socks, heavy jumpers and jogging bottoms. There were quite a few people already in the sea, and some had woolly hats on. It was a friendly and welcoming image, seeing these colourful bobbled knitted hats bopping up and down. After introducing me to a few members of The Blue Tits, we stripped off to our swimwear. The last thing I wanted to do was remove my clothes and wear the bare minimum – it required some level of insanity.

The sea was calm, as if it was cajoling me with its serenity: it's OK to come in.

Tess held my hand as we stood by the edge of the shore and looked out towards the horizon. We then turned to look at each other and laughed at the whole insanity of what we were about to do. Every cell in my body screamed for me to turn back. It went against all my instincts to step any closer to the sea. I was already freezing. I held Tess's hand tight and she squeezed it: I'm here, close to you. I wanted to turn back, though I never said. I wanted to go back to the comfort of The Long Barn with its open fire and cuddle up to Truffle and Blackberry. I was out of my comfort zone. I had always been fearful of the sea; it was a living, breathing mystery that humans had only scratched the surface of. It was bigger than us.

I didn't like New Year's Eve – the societal pressure to do something, to be somewhere other than where we already stood. In my twenties I had embraced it; I danced in clubs and drank in raucous bars. As I got older, I always willed it to come and go quietly. I could feel time slipping through my fingers. We never really measure time, because if we did, we wouldn't all be so guilty of wasting it. And now the new year meant that the distance between myself and my mother was getting greater. I was leaving her behind, a series of years between us; icebergs drifting apart.

The last New Year's Eve I spent with my mother was in 2013, when we clinked our glasses and welcomed in 2014. My mother sat wearing a blue scarf and said: 'This time next year I won't have cancer and we'll celebrate properly! And all my hair would've grown!' In actuality, it was the day we buried her. We had clinked our glasses to the unknown. American philosopher William James said: 'No fact in human nature is more characteristic than its willingness to live on a chance.'

'I'm here with you,' Tess said as we gingerly took a step closer to the sea, a temperamental and sage entity; Tess and I, little girls holding hands entering a mysterious and unknown realm.

'Now, we're not supposed to stay in too long, and it's your first time. We'll be in for a few minutes and then out. You'll be fine, Lovely.'

My feet submerged into the freezing-cold water. In what felt like seconds, my ankle bones felt a searing pain – as if someone had taken a hammer to them. As we walked further in, my breathing changed: short, sharp, a staccato of breaths; uncontrollable breathing.

'Kiran, breathe in and out gently. Control your breathing.' Tess was still holding my hand.

When the freezing water reached my chest, I was certain it

would cave in. My breathing became erratic again. I had never felt so cold since the day of my mother's funeral. As I stood in the freezing sea, I remembered standing at the burial on that cold, miserable New Year's Eve: a world gone wrong. The burial ground was frozen; a hard, impervious earth where nothing would ever grow. It was the coldest day that I had ever lived in. I wanted to scream as they lowered her body to the ground. But I stood still, frozen, mute. Never had I felt so much but said so little.

'URGH! IT'S SO COLD!!' I screamed.

'Do you want to leave, Lovely? We don't need to stay any longer.'

'No! I want to stay!!!'

My body was held in the grasp of shock: the shock of entering a foreign liquid space. I had lost my footing from walking on eroded and arid land. It was shock that was wrapped in the cries of newborn babies entering the world. It was the shock of life. Shock can reverberate forever. I dropped Tess's hand and dived into the sea and started to swim. My neck so cold, I thought it would break. I could hear Tess shout my name; it sounded as if I had left her in another room, in another world, in another life. I took long and wide strokes and swam out to the deepest parts of me; away from myself and towards myself. It wasn't just the Irish Sea that swallowed me, it was the Celtic Sea that joined it, and then the North Atlantic: an interconnected world. I felt the wholeness, the oneness of this space, planet, Earth. I was disappearing into this otherness that had frightened me for so long. These were the seas that I would never swim in: too cold; too bleak; too other.

I stopped swimming and raised my head out of the water.

'Kiran! Are you OK?!' Tess was still standing where I had left her.

I'm fine!' I could hardly speak; I could hardly breathe.

'What happened?!' Tess was 30 metres away from me.

'I'm sorry, I didn't mean to frighten you!'

I swam back to her.

'I can't believe you took off like that. Straight in there! You did it! Your first swim in the sea in the UK!'

'Sorry for going for so long.'

'Don't be silly, you took no time at all. Do you notice something?'

'What?'

'We're not shivering.'

Tess was right. It was still cold, but it no longer pained us. Winter sun shone on our faces. We made our way back to our bags; it was time to go.

'Can I ask you something?' Tess said. 'What made you think you'd been gone ages?'

'Because I have. I've been gone a long time.'

40

WILF'S WALK

One fine spring afternoon in March, I decided to take a different walk to the one that I normally took. My usual walk had started to feel prosaic; it was time to change direction. I remembered Wilf said he walked every evening on a route that was the opposite direction to mine. I decided to walk his chosen path. Instead of turning left at the T-junction with the Roman road, he turned right. He passed the cattle grid and headed towards the Highland cows. I had only ever driven that route, never walked. So one afternoon, I turned right instead of left.

I had walked past Wilf on my way up to the T-junction. I could see he was busy filling up water containers, so I just waved and carried on walking. I then stopped and shouted. 'Hey, Wilf! I'm taking your route today for my walk!' He couldn't hear me, so I walked towards him. 'Today, I'm doing your evening walk.' He laughed as if he had always been waiting for me to tell him that. 'Yes, it's a lovely walk and it's a lovely day for it. The view from up there is magnificent! And where's your red coat?' It was too warm to wear my Little Red Riding Hood raincoat. I had wondered if I'd be unrecognisable without it. 'I'd better go, Wilf. See you soon!'

There seemed to be more butterflies this year I thought as I turned right. I had passed quite a few and stopped to look at them and admire their markings. I tuned into the sound of the countryside: birds, bees, farm animals, insects. Whoever said the countryside was quiet?! I could hear life so lucidly; the smallest of tremors. The only thing I couldn't hear was the pigeon that had nested in my head. I'm not quite sure when it left; some things enter and leave our lives with much fanfare, while others enter and leave imperceptibly.

On the right of me I passed the gate that would take me up to the cairn that Tess and I had gone up last autumn. I smiled at the memory of it: the wind that had stolen our voices but had blown new life into us.

I could see I would soon reach the top where the road would flatten out. I felt excited; I was reaching its summit. I didn't want to rush towards it. I wanted to take in the view, the new growth of ferns and wild flowers. This walk was more barren than my walk; there weren't that many trees, just a wider and more open terrain. Ancient dry stone walls bordered the road. Yellow, orange and pale yellow daffodils were scattered around the verges on the bases of the walls. This walk was far more remote than the walk I was used to. This really was the wilds of Wales.

I reached the top where the road flattened. On the right of me was an ancient wall, but on the left was a panoramic view of the whole landscape; a wide and expansive sea of green. The landscape opened up like a fan. This was the view Wilf told me about. I could hear his words: 'Most evenings I walk right up to the top of the valley. I look down and everything looks small and far away. And I feel like I'm on top of the world.'

I sat down cross-legged on the grass and surrendered to the beauty of it all, just like I did as a ten-year-old in school assembly, except this was no collage – this was real. It was like the ocean on New Year's Eve: it swallowed me. The hills seemed to be draped in solemnity. Everything that existed at the bottom of the hills, the odd farmhouse and barn, looked fragile and insignificant. I took out a nectarine from my rucksack and bit into it.

As I basked in the majesty of the view in front of me, a thought entered my head. Perhaps life wasn't a giant puzzle that needed to be solved? Perhaps it was something that just needed to be felt? There is no shame in allowing our hearts to break, to break in great visions of natural beauty, in song lyrics, over the books we have read, over sunrises and sunsets, and when we have lost the people we love. It's in these moments, when we allow ourselves to be shipwrecked, that we really come alive, even though we may feel dead. We are meant to feel. After all, *a life half-felt is a life half-lived*.

My mother now belonged in this timeless place of space and time, this framing of life, so nebulous and impalpable. Nature doesn't ask for permission; it just exists, and we must accept it. It doesn't care whether we like it or not or about any wishes we may have. And I was happy to surrender to it. I had been on my knees for so long over things that really didn't matter much in the end or things that I shouldn't have cared about so much for. The things that did matter would never leave me. No matter how much we try to escape things, some places and people never leave us, and we leave bits of us in those places; like a favourite book or scarf. And like handkerchiefs, the people we love live in our breast pockets close to our heart. And we wear them well.

'Mum, isn't this beautiful?' I said aloud, willing her to hear me. 'This is where I live now. It's not forever, because nothing ever is, but it's where I am right now. It's all been rather hellish since you died. I know you won't quite believe it, and you will probably laugh, "What's a city girl like you doing in the middle of nowhere?" But if you've lost your direction in life, it doesn't matter where you are. I couldn't look after dad. I tried, but he lost himself, as we all did. But you probably already know that.'

I stood up and looked down; everything appeared so small and so far away. And then I heard it, a sound that had once been unfamiliar to me, only this time I knew what it was. It was the sound of the cuckoo – the cuckoo had arrived once again! I couldn't wait to tell Wilf.

My heart swelled with gratitude from looking at a new perspective. I felt a sense of contentment gazing at the green hills, the same kind of contentment one may get from seeing a Monet or a Picasso. There were no neon lights or signs of the city, no sounds that told me something was an emergency. Wilf knew this land like the back of his hand, but for me, it was the road less travelled.

ACKNOWLEDGEMENTS

Thank you to my new friends for their warmth and generosity of spirit: Donna, Andy, Sarah, Glen, Rod, Tess, Andrew, Hara, Grenville, Wilf, Jane, Dai and Miar.

Thank you to my old friends for sitting with me in the dark and the light: Alicia Buller, Poonam Kanda, Esther King, Sophia Hratsous, Stephanie Lam, Jo Bowd, Roberta Podavitte, Frank Ryan, Graham Brough, Sofia Brough and Dave Evans.

Thank you for family love: Michael Sohotra, Violet Sohotra, Jason Sohotra, Selina Sohotra-Clarke, Nasib Gill, Sheila Gill, Sonia Gill and Peter Gill.

Thank you Nigel Warburton for your encouragement.

Thank you Christian Cargill and Lily Wakeley for turning my article into a Tribeca-award-winning film! What a trip!

My Twitter family – I thank you for your love and support.

Thanks to Nicola Crane from Octopus Publishing for being such a wonderful editor, and thank you to the whole team involved in putting this book together.

Thanks to my agent, David Godwin, for your guidance.

Thanks to *The Guardian* newspaper for publishing my articles.

Thank you to the village of Cellan and the people of Wales for their wonderful Welsh hospitality.

A special thanks to Simon for keeping all my broken parts safe.

ABOUT THE AUTHOR

Kiran Sidhu is a freelance journalist and has written features, and lifestyle and opinion pieces for *The Guardian*, *The Observer*, *The i*, *The Telegraph*, *The Independent*, *Metro*, *Woman* magazine, *Woman's Own* and *Breathe* magazine. Her article about her farmer friend Wilf was the 13th most read article on *The Guardian* website in 2021, and was made into short documentary, *Heart Valley*, directed by Christian Cargill and written by Kiran Sidhu. *Heart Valley* was made available by *The New Yorker* and the BBC, and went on to win Best Documentary Short at Tribeca Film Festival. Kiran Sidhu lives in the Welsh valleys with her husband.

Kiransidhu.co.uk
KiranSidhu41